Transformed by Justice that Forgives, Heals & Restores

A Guide to for Long-Term Prisoners to Challenge Your Thinking, Help You Move Forward to a Life Having Value, Purpose and Hope---and Become that Better Person You are Called to Be

Rick Trencavel

Deveron Books

"We must learn to regard people less in terms of what they do or omit to do, and more in the light of what they suffer".

Dietrich Bonhoeffer,

Lutheran Pastor and Nazi Prisoner, 1941

Deveron Books
Additional copies available at Amazon.com for a modest cost

ISBN: 978-1-77835-299-7

Printed in the United States of America

Contents

Part 4: The Part of the Gospel that Relates to the Transformation of People----"The Things Concerning the Name of Jesus Christ"

Part 5: The Part of the Gospel Dealing With the Things Concerning the Kingdom of God--- the Future Destiny of the Earth and Your Place in It

Introduction

I wrote this book for people that often feel they have little positive hope in their lives because I recognize how important hope is in a person's life when they are dealing with the opposite of hope-----despair.

This is how I felt at a time in my life when my 8 year old son was killed by a pickup truck in an accident while riding on his bicycle outside our rural home. Despair took over my life for a period following this tragic event.

Likewise, many people in prison serving long terms of imprisonment may experience periods with little sense of hope and instead, despair sets in with nothing to look forward to and every day being the same.

While I have never been in prison, and I have no credibility on that front, **I can relate to feelings of despair**, which fortunately in time I was able to overcome.

The sense of hopelessness and despair felt by some prisoners was brought home to me in a number of books I have read but one book in particular impressed me for its proposed way to help overcome these feelings. It was written by Charles Colson, who was sent to prison for his part in the Watergate scandal during the presidency of Richard Nixon back in 1975. After he was released, he wrote a book some twenty-two years ago called ***Justice That Restores*** that dealt with changes involving "restorative justice" that he felt were the best way forward for persons sent to prison by the criminal justice system. (The concept of *restorative justice* is mentioned briefly later in this introduction and discussed in further detail later in the book).

This book builds on some of the concepts he introduced with a particular focus on those serving long terms of imprisonment because longer term prisoners face a separate set of challenges.

So, while I have not personally experienced these particular challenges, I have read the thoughts of current and former prisoners who have detailed these things. I have corresponded with several long-term prisoners for over 12 years, one serving LWOP from age 18, and one serving 30 years to life from age 20. I have learned a lot from them. Based on what I have read from others with first-hand experience, here are some of the challenges as I understand them, that longer term prisoners face.

But let me first discuss just what **long-term** imprisonment is. The average life span for males in the USA is currently about 78 years. If we assume a person becomes an adult around age 18, then that gives the average male about 60 years of adult life. Hence, ***anything greater or equal to 15 years of being in prison--1/4 of an adult lifespan----- would be considered long-term imprisonment.***

This book is meant particularly for prisoners who have spent or will spend at least ***15 or more years in prison.*** Such prisoners face special challenges that prisoners with shorter terms do not face, particularly mental and emotional challenges.

These include feelings of loneliness, an unchanging boring routine of "a life without action", and a sense of despair that comes with having to spend a long time in prison.

Not only must long-term prisoners cope with all the day to day unpleasantness of prison like every prisoner------almost total control over your life by others, lack of respect, being deprived of the many things that make life enjoyable, fear of assaults, an inability to trust or confide in others, experiencing other inmates getting released while they are left stuck in prison, and so on----but the lack of positive hope for the foreseeable future can add to a cycle of despair.

The purpose of this book then is to try to do the following:

- To convince you that you are not a write-off or a reject of society, but that you have real value as a human being and that your life can have meaning and purpose, even in prison.
- To encourage you to explore a better way forward---that you don't have to forever remain the person you were when you committed the crimes that sent you to prison.
- To convince you that you were put on this Earth for a good purpose----a purpose only you can fulfill, and then to seek out and take hold of that purpose.
- To help give you a context or "worldview" that explains why people do bad things and why, despite this, our world is eventually going to move towards a very positive future----a future you can be a part of.
- To encourage you to explore pathways for forgiveness following the concept of **restorative justice**, which focuses on **healing** of ***all the parties*** affected by a crime----the victim(s), the offender, and the community-----rather than focusing just on punishment of the offender. (see chapters 29 and 30)

The aim of restorative justice ***for the offender*** is to enable him to come to terms with his criminal past, to acknowledge the harm he caused to others, and then to help him move on in his life in a more positive way. These things are necessary so that forgiveness, healing, and the restoration of his self-worth as a valued human being can take place.

These concepts----forgiveness, healing and restoration, are part of the Christian worldview. **The Christian worldview allows a person to be forgiven of any past mistake and to have a fresh start; it allows wrongdoing from a person's past to be put behind them so that it no longer dominates their thinking about who they are and their worth as a human being**.

My interest is ***in the person's situation as it is now*** and offers hope for their future. I am not interested in dwelling on things in their past **because we can't change tha**t. But we can change our thinking, feelings and mental outlook as it is now.

This is a long book----because the aim is to help you **move your thinking in a more positive direction---and that takes time**. This book has 48 chapters that each take about 10 minutes to read. The aim is that you will read this book and reflect on it --- **one chapter per day for 48 days.**

The first chapter is about your life ***as it is now***. It may be a bit of a downer so don't be put off by this. It is my way of letting you know that I have empathy for some of things you may be having to deal with in prison. The purpose of the first chapter is to lay the groundwork for what follows in the book, so that you might explore changing your thinking in a more positive direction.

Even if reading this book doesn't appeal to you just now, I hope you will keep it because it may interest you later, and, above all, I hope you will find it of some help in coping with your imprisonment.

- Rick Trencavel, Deveron Books

Part 1: Dealing with the Challenges You Face as a Longer-term Prisoner

Day 1 - Chapter 1: Negative Thinking: The Challenges You Have to Deal With Every Day That Can Drag You Down

This book is a book about HOPE and about Finding that Good Purpose of Why You Were Put here on Planet Earth. As mentioned in the Introduction, it is written particularly for prisoners who have spent or must spend many long years in prison before there is any hope of being released, or who face the prospect of never leaving prison.

Your current situation is definitely not the fulfillment of that good purpose as to why you were put on this Earth. Instead, it is a sad detour where you moved away from that purpose, but it is still only that-----a *detour.* It is not the end of your story or your destiny.

This chapter reviews some of the bad conditions and negative thinking you may have to put up with every day and that drags you down. But let me repeat-----I have never been to prison so I have no direct experience or credibility on this issue. The challenges I list are only based on the experiences shared by others in letters or from books, articles,and other internet sources such as Quora---an internet question and answer site where former prison inmates share their stories.

The descriptions that follow may or may not be things you have experienced. They are listed to show that I recognize there are negative challenges you have to contend with.

These may include putting up day in day out with people you don't want to be around, in an environment you don't like, with many petty rules, waiting for endless counts, slow wait lines for just about everything, and control by others over virtually everything you do. This routine gets "old" very fast.

For some, you don't "live"----you "exist" in a world of boring routines, lousy food, poor medical and dental attention, and a life that is devoid of action. Even meaningful conversation is hard to come by.

And every day is basically like every other day. Time stands still while your family and friends outside move on. Every man needs to feel his life has a purpose but what purpose or meaning can there be under these conditions when you face years of boring routine?

You can go for years without experiencing a hug, or even a kind word from another human being including family members. Over time, friends abandon you and family visits or letters and emails become less and less frequent and finally dry up completely. For many in this situation, it often seems nobody seems to care whether you are alive or dead. You are alone and completely on your own.

It is likely you are periodically stripped of your humanity and dignity through things like strip-searches, or the dumping and destruction of your personal property during a shakedown. You may even be humiliated by being shackled and strip-searched every time you leave your cell.

And some say that prison life can wear you down because of the constant noise and the lack of calmness and privacy. All these things may numb you to the normal positive human emotions. What's worse, you must typically maintain a hard outer face that forces you to suppress positive feelings for your fellow man.

Depending on your situation, fear may always be present so that you must be constantly on guard for the unexpected. This forces you to present a hard, uncaring, and indifferent attitude to those around you---a "f--k the world" attitude.

It may not be a matter of choice, but a matter of **survival.** In addition, you typically can't afford to let any perceived slight to be forgiven or go unchallenged. To do so would make you appear weak and open you to further challenges.

For some, you may have been a victim of degrading sexual violence or gang rape when you first came to jail or prison that stripped you of your manhood.

These negative things may cause a prisoner to feel he has no control over his life and that he has little value as a human being. And all these negative things can cause health problems that are often not dealt with in prison.

Given all these negative conditions, it is not surprising that a 2016 study by Prison Policy Initiative shows that each year in prison reduces a prisoner's lifespan by up to 2 years (although a prisoner can partly recovery from this once he is released and has fully completed his parole).

This is because of what are often appalling prison conditions (like no air-conditioning, and poor access to needed healthcare, lack of fresh fruit and vegetables in the prison diet, boredom, a common condition where a prisoner feels no sense of purpose, and general loneliness). All these things explain why imprisonment is definitely a form of suffering and should be greatly reduced.

If it were not for friendships with other prisoners and a daily routine, you might question whether this life is really worth living. But even with prison friendships, --- in the final analysis, you can trust no one.

When you first came to prison, you may have denied that this was really happening to you. You probably went through a kind of grieving process even if you didn't realize it, for the loss of all the things you had to give up- --hanging out with friends and family, cars, riding motorcycles, fast food restaurants, sunsets, pizza, a cold beer, trips to the beach, even little things like sitting on the can in private, or choosing your own clothing.

All these have become memories. More and more, you are on your own and alone. The free world fades---as something experienced by others, something you see only on television.

In fact, the few friendships you do make are temporary at best because the state can transfer you or your friends to another institution at any time, and the loyalty of "friends" is ultimately only to themselves, not to you when it comes to a crunch.

You may also have had to deal with feelings of shame and guilt. During the first few years of being locked up, you probably hoped for a legal miracle----an appeal that would be successful, or some new evidence would come to light that would call into question the verdict. Inmate "lawyers" may have helped you keep this form of hope alive, but as you know all too well, it usually brings little or no relief.

You may still feel you were unfairly treated by the criminal justice system at your trial because you were given a court-appointed lawyer who was incompetent or cared little about your defense. You may have been young and felt everyone was against you and didn't take your particular circumstances into account. Or, the actual criminal charges may have been more serious than you think you deserved or the sentence much harsher----given your age at the time.

As a result, you may have lashed out in anger about the way you were treated by the justice system, or tried to escape and ended up in lockdown status. If it didn't happen to you, you've likely seen it happen to others.

You look around you and see prisoners who have been locked up for 15, 25, or 40 years. Many of them have a sullen stare as if they are looking at nothing, and they walk with a shuffle as if they are going nowhere----almost like they feel emotionally dead inside. You think, "Man, is that what I'm going to be like? Is this what I am becoming or will feel like in time?"

You may have gotten covered with prison tattoos to relieve the boredom and to help you to fit in to the prison scene. After all, who cares if you get covered in ink? Why not?

In fact, you may ask yourself, "Does anyone really care what happens to me? Would it matter to anyone? Even if I am eventually released, how will I exist if I have no money, no family who care, minimal education, no valid job experience, no usable job skills, and having lots of visible prison tattoos that label me as a convicted felon? Will I end up broke all the time and moving from spot to spot, living in shabby rooming houses or homeless men's shelters? Will I be able to control my addiction problems? How will I exist and what kind of life will that be?"

And then you think, never mind the future, what about now? This isn't 'living' so do I really want to put up with all this for many years to come? Is this all that life has to offer or ever will offer? You may even have thought, "Would I be better off dead?"

And you have probably thought, what lies beyond this life? Something good, something bad or utter oblivion and nothingness? Is it all pointless?

You may have been able to relate many things we have mentioned in this chapter-----about your life as it is now. But is this the end of your life story?

Not at all. It is simply another chapter in your life journey. **It does not mean your life has no purpose or meaning.**

You can make changes in your thinking that make you a better person----much different from the one you were when you were arrested.

One such person who did this was John Newton, a hated slave trader in the mid-1700's who made his living transporting slaves who had been kidnapped in Africa and brought to the New World to be enslaved and treated not as human beings but as property. He was responsible for the beatings and deaths of many of these enslaved people as he transported them. To polite English society, he was regarded as the 'lowest of the low'.

But about age 30, he realized he had never grasped hold of the true purpose why the Eternal One had put him here on this planet. He finally woke up, changed his thinking and actions and grasped hold of that purpose----to help others who were in the same bad way that he had been.

He changed course and contributed greatly to ending slavery in the British Empire and wrote the hymn that has inspired millions of people—"Amazing Grace".

The first verse of this hymn expresses his gratitude to God for opening his eyes to the good purpose why he was put on this earth.

Amazing Grace, how sweet the sound,
That saved a wretch like me.
I once was lost but now am found,
Was blind, but now I see.

T'was Grace that taught my heart to fear
And Grace, my fears relieved
How precious did that Grace appear
The hour I first believed.

Through many dangers, toils and snares
I have already come;
'Tis Grace that brought me safe thus far
and Grace will lead me home.

If a man like John Newton----a man so despised and written off as a hopeless case could get his life back on track so that he could fulfill his true purpose----then so can you. There are no hopeless cases with God, the Eternal Lord of the Universe, unless a person wants that outcome.

It is possible to leave the - "blindness" that John Newton talked about when he wrote "Amazing Grace" and embrace a new vision that fulfills the purpose that God intended for you and that gives you hope for the future.

He chose not to remain locked in his past----a choice you can also make.

Day 2 - Chapter 2: You Were Put on this Earth for a Good Purpose----*You Just Need to Seek it out!*

God had a good purpose for bringing **you** into being here on Earth and **that good purpose is still intact and waiting for you to seek it and grasp hold of it.** With God there are no hopeless cases---no people who are write-offs---no " worst of the worst".

What the Eternal Lord of the Universe wants is for you to seek out that good purpose He has for you and then grasp hold of it----the good purpose He has always wanted for you. **It won't come if you don't do something to seek it out.**

And, He isn't focused on your past because He knows you can't change that. **He is focused on your present and future thinking and outlook**---which you ***can*** influence.

What He wants is for you to **learn from your past** and consider changing the direction of your life with a different outlook and view of the world. He is interested in what you are going to do starting NOW and in the future to pursue that good purpose He has always wanted for you. To do this, you need to gain insight into a number of things including:

1. The root cause why things went downhill for you so that you ended up in prison.

2. A description of just what His good purpose for human beings actually is, both now and in the future----here on Earth.

3. What you can do to help you get in tune with that good purpose He has always wanted for you. This new path will allow you to move forward in a more positive way.

4. Some prisoners appear to feel no guilt or sense of remorse, and seem to be forever emotionally disconnected from the person or family they victimized. This may happen because they feel they have no value as human beings and have been rejected or cut-off by family, friends, and society. This presents a bigger challenge to overcome but it still comes down to one main thing: **Changing your thinking in the way you view the world.**

You can start a new path to fulfill that good purpose God still has always had for you. He is simply waiting for you to explore and seek it out. There is no downside. You have nothing to lose and everything to gain.

Day 3 - Chapter 3 : Guilt and Shame---Ways to Help Deal with these Negative Emotions and Promote Healing

When a person is sent to prison for serious crimes, he may have intense negative feelings of guilt and shame. He may feel shame for letting down his own family and experience guilt for the hurt, loss, and disruption he caused to other families. How he feels may be something like this: "*My family doesn't deserve being labeled because of what I did. This is not what my family stands for.*"

These feelings may come about at a sentencing hearing that applies some type of negative label to the offender. Any such label only relates to your past, not your future----because **every living human being has the potential to make meaningful changes in their thinking and behavior.**

The human mind can change and is flexible. What is needed is the will and encouragement to move your thinking in a different direction. You do not have to remain stuck with the thinking that dominated you when your crimes took place and that may still influence your thinking in prison.

That is what **healing** and **restorative justice** is all about----one of the dominant themes we will explore in this book.

While we can't change the past, every person can move his thinking and actions in a different direction----***now and in the future***. That allows every one of us to come to terms with his past, and seek forgiveness for past wrongdoing.

So, let's begin by talking about these two feelings-----**guilt** and **shame**. We will deal first with guilt, which is the less harmful one and can even be a good thing at times.

Guilt

Guilt occurs when we recognize that we have done something wrong or inappropriate---something that doesn't match up with the values we were taught (by our parents, teachers, Sunday school teachers, etc.), or with society's values.

Guilt is the awareness of a failure on our part when measured against some standard such as the Ten Commandments.

Guilt tells us, "I have done a bad thing."

But, guilt itself isn't a bad thing ***because it shows our conscience is working*** for us because it makes us aware we have done something wrong, something that caused hurt to others.

Guilt ***brings on an uncomfortable feeling***-- - psychological discomfort---that can cause us to recognize wrongdoing, apologize for it, and then motivate us to make some meaningful changes.

Hence, **guilt can often be a positive influence when it prompts us to change our thinking and behavior**.

What is the opposite of guilt? The opposite of feeling guilt is having a clear conscience**----**where we feel no discomfort for something we have done.

What is the remedy for overcoming feelings of guilt? It is ***forgiveness***-----forgiveness of our actions by a Higher Being, and, *if* ***possible***, by those directly affected by our actions, and lastly, by ourself.

In a Christian context, this means as a first step, **to acknowledge----both to God and to those harmed by our actions----that we did something wrong and hurtful.** That is, we must be willing to admit that we violated some moral standard. In so doing, **we**

take personal ownership for what happened---for what landed us in prison. We must also be willing to accept that we deserved to be sent to prison for the harm we caused so that justice could be seen to be done----for the sake of the victims of the crime.

To obtain forgiveness, we must genuinely recognize the hurt we caused to others by ***declaring regret in a public way*** to those affected by our actions. This is usually called expressing remorse.

If we can't feel any sense of the pain we caused another family or even to our own family for what happened, then we will usually feel no need for forgiveness.

Some prison inmates suffer from a mental illness disorder called Anti-social Personality Disorder (or ASPD for short). These prisoners often feel no guilt, no shame, and no sense of remorse and appear to be completely emotionally disconnected from the people they victimized. This presents a bigger challenge to be overcome but it still comes down to one main thing: **Trying to change old harmful thinking patterns.**

If we can be open and serious about making changes to our thinking and behavior, then God is willing to forgive us regardless of the nature or seriousness of the crimes in our past.

Forgiveness allows us to experience the removal of the guilt feelings for our past actions. It is like we are starting with a clean slate.

This in turn allows us to move forward with a more positive outlook and self-image.

And the Higher Power we call God will forgive us if we genuinely commit to changing our thinking and outlook-----even if the victims of our crimes (or their families), won't.

This is the message that Jesus taught us--- **that we are not forever tied to our past but can move beyond the things in our life that we cannot change**----if we are willing to acknowledge the bad things we were responsible for and work at moving our thinking and actions in a different direction.

Let us now turn our attention to shame, which is both a more complex feeling and more difficult one to deal with.

Shame

Shame is an intensely painful feeling or experience where we come to believe that *we are seriously flawed*. Shame says, "I *feel badly about who I am*". Guilt tells us, "**I *made*** *a bad mistake*" whereas shame says, "**I *am*** *a mistake.*"

Shame can make us feel unworthy of love, or unworthy of connection with other people, or unworthy of acceptance by other people including our own family or the community where we grew up. **Shame says** to us, "*The only human connection you deserve is with other rapists, murderers, child molesters, etc.* ***in prison***. These are the only people you are fit to have connection with."

So, feelings of shame directly impact our relationships with others.

In its religious aspect, shame also says, "I *am not worthy of God's love and care. I am a 'bad seed'-- a child of Hell'.* This is completely false thinking. This is true **only if that is what you want to believe----and choose to be**.

The only type of person who never experiences shame is a person who can't feel any regret, sadness, or other bad feelings for the harm he caused other people.

However, sometimes, what appears to be a "lack of remorse" at a sentencing hearing is something quite different----*the offender* ***is so overwhelmed in the court room by what is happening to him*** *that he has real difficulty expressing how badly he feels for what he did and may even show a nervous smile.*

This then gets interpreted that he has no feelings for the family of the victim and is incapable of showing remorse even *when this is clearly* ***not how he feels***. The offender may be just stressed and overwhelmed by anxiety at the court proceedings.

What is the opposite of shame? The opposite of a feeling of shame is *receiving honor or being honored by other people*. When we are honored by others for something we have done, we feel very good about ourselves as a human being. It boosts our sense of self-worth and makes us feel valuable to those around us. For example, a fireman might be honored for going into a blazing house to save a child.

Here are some other characteristics of shame that researchers such as Brene Brown have determined:

For a person to feel shame, he must first have a mental image of a model person or group of persons he looks up to.

This ***ideal self*** then becomes the standard we use when we make comparisons with our own self-image and what we are really like. When we fall far short of the ideal, we feel shame.

Shame involves a complete loss of faith in who you really are in comparison with the ideal person you would like to be. If you do something or become someone you feel would be rejected by this "ideal" group, then shame is the result.

Shame may also result from bad feelings towards you by people you know----your family, former friends or colleagues, and people in your community. Here are some examples:

- Shame at being labelled a convicted felon or an exconvict when you are released from prison and return to your community.

- For men there are some added burdens surrounding shame that are often driven by the attitudes of society. Shame is felt when you fail at something and other people are aware of it.

- You may feel shame when other inmates think you can be pushed around. This lack of respect is degrading and shameful. It makes you feel like a zero.

- Shame can result from showing any weakness. Hence an inmate will often do anything necessary to avoid being seen as being fearful, vulnerable or disrespected even if it means being put in a segregation unit for an extended period of time. This can cause a lot of anxiety for an inmate.

All these things can result in feelings of real intense mental pain that can be very negative.

Unlike guilt, which can have a positive effect, **feelings of shame are usually destructive** because they undermine the very part of us that believes we can change, do better, and be a better person.

Shame says that I am a failed human being-----a person who is not worthy of acceptance and who should be shut away from society.

That is why shame is so destructive. It can make us feel emotionally and spiritually dead inside even though we are biologically alive. This can lead to a person withdrawing and becoming isolated from other people or becoming bitter, depressed, suicidal, or wanting to blame others and lash out.

Researcher Brene Brown says, "*It is human nature to want to feel worthy of love and belonging. When we experience shame, we feel disconnected and desperate for worthiness. When we're hurting, either full of shame or even just feeling the fear of shame, we are more likely to engage in self-destructive behaviors and to attack or shame others.*" Brown, B. (2012, March 16) *Listening to Shame* [Video] TED Conferences. https://www.ted.com/talks/brene_brown_listening to shame

Is Feeling *Shame* the same as Feeling *Humiliation*?

No. People typically believe they deserve shame whereas they do not believe they deserve humiliation. For example, if a person's self-talk says, "I'm a loser and a failure as a human being", that is shame. ***It's all about me as a failed human being.*** This may cause a person to "shut down, act out, or fight back" because he thinks there is no other way out for him.

But, if a person feels unfairly humiliated by a boss or some other person, they will say, "My boss is out of control. I ***don't deserve this***." The person knows this is really about an abusive boss and not about himself.

When we feel humiliated, we usually still relate to our values and this may prompt us to look for strategies to deal with the humiliation.

Hence, **feelings of shame are much more harmful to a person than feelings of humiliation.** While some prisoners feel no shame, **most do**----at least at some point----**for letting others down**. In the next chapter we will explore ways to help deal with the problem of shame.

Questions to Think About

1. Have you experienced guilt feelings after committing a criminal act? Have these feelings gone away or are they a burden you still carry with you?

2. Have you experienced shame after being convicted of a crime and sent to prison? What did it feel like? Why did you feel shame? Have these feelings gone away or have they stayed with you?

Day 4 - Chapter 4: The Bigger Challenge: Overcoming Feelings of Shame

As we discussed in the last chapter, shame is usually a very negative feeling and can be destructive to a person, particularly if it hangs around.

What does researcher Brene Brown recommend we do about it? (Again, we recognize that some prisoners suffering from ASPD---Antisocial Personality Disorder, a recognized mental disorder----may be unable to experience feelings of guilt or shame- --and this is an added challenge in their thinking that must be worked on and hopefully overcome.)

Prof. Brown says, "*If we can share our story with someone who responds with empathy and understanding, then shame can't survive. Shame is a social wound and needs a social remedy*". (Brown, Brene. *Listening to Shame* [Video] *TED* March 16, 2012, https:// www.tcd.com/talks/brene_brown _listening to shame)

Therefore, she recommends that a person feeling shame tries to ***adopt strategies to help cope with shame***. How does a person go about this? What strategies does she recommend?

1. **Try to find someone who can express empathy** for you----someone who can put themselves in your shoes and feel your pain.

While this may not be easy in the context of prison it may be possible with some relatives, friends, or even some fellow prisoners.

When you receive empathy from another person, it opens the way for **acceptance** and **social re-connection**. Why? Because when a person empathizes with us they can relate to what we feel-----**this validation and acceptance of our feelings gives us permission to reconnect socially and let go of our shame.** (Note: feeling empathy is not the same as feeling sympathy. Sympathy says, "I feel sorry for you," whereas empathy says, "I can relate to how you are feeling.")

Nor does feeling empathy for you by another person mean they are dismissing or ignoring the pain and suffering that you may have caused to others. But, **they are validating that your feelings, as a fellow human being, are legitimate.**

Another strategy is to practice **self-compassion** . She says, "**When we are able to be gentle with ourselves** *in the midst of shame, we're more likely to reach out, connect and experience empathy,*" (instead of lashing out and blaming others). It is easier to be gentle with ourselves if another person expresses empathy for us and accepts how we feel as being legitimate.

From a spiritual perspective, Jesus is a model for how we should deal with people who are experiencing Guilt and Shame. (We already have discussed how the **remedy for guilt** is **forgiveness** and we know the Bible has much to say about that topic. It is the ultimate reason why Jesus died for our sins.)

In the New Testament, shame is mentioned in passing but is not treated as a specific item. It is often implied even when not specifically mentioned. For example, there is no doubt that the Apostle Peter felt intense shame when he realized that he had denied even knowing Jesus three times following Jesus' arrest. The same is true of Judas, who betrayed Jesus to the Romans for 30 pieces of silver, and then went out and hanged himself.

Likewise the woman arrested for committing adultery was undoubtedly feeling intense shame when she was caught in the act by the Jewish religious authorities. They wanted to condemn her to death by stoning, but Jesus refused to condemn her.

Instead, he told the religious authorities, "*He that is without sin, let him cast the first stone.*"

Another hated person, Zacchaeus, a corrupt tax collector and collaborator with the Roman authorities, probably had feelings of both guilt and shame for his actions when he met up with Jesus, but Jesus was willing to sit down and have a meal with him.

So how did Jesus deal with these people who were experiencing feelings of shame? **Did he shun them so that he would not be linked to their deeds or lifestyle**?

No, he sat down with some of the them at a meal, and interacted with them in a way that showed he accepted them as **valued human beings.**

He did not confront them in an "in your face" judgmental way. Nor did he excuse or ignore the bad things they had done.

Rather, he **gently nudged them in a positive way to make changes in their life.** He told Zacchaeus, the hated dishonest tax collector, that he was coming to his house for a meal. To meet with someone over a meal was a sign of social acceptance.

Likewise, he had a **non-judgmental discussion** with the woman taken in adultery. When he told her accusers, "*Let he who is without sin cast the first stone*", the religious authorities backed off and that was the end of it.

In all these cases, he showed these individuals that they were persons worthy of his attention. **This sent them a message of social acceptance-----**that their lives mattered and had value----something they desperately needed to hear to ease the pain of their shame.

So, the initial remedy for shame is ***acceptance*****----**acceptance by others so that we feel we have value as a member of the community----one who is worthy of connection with other people and also worthy of God's love and care.

This is the approach Jesus took. It was only people full of pride and hypocrisy like the Pharisees that refused to change, that he took a different approach with.

This same approach is also the message he taught in the parable of the Lost Son. The prodigal or "lost" son had shamed his family by squandering the inheritance money he demanded his father give him even though his father was still alive. His father reluctantly agreed. Once he obtained the money from his father, he went to another country and spent it all on prostitutes and partying.

Soon the inheritance money was all gone and he had nothing to live on. When he was on the point of starving, he decided to go back home and seek his father's mercy and forgiveness. When he got near to his home, his father ***ran out to meet*** *him and* accepted him back with joy by hugging him----even without knowing his son's changed thinking at that point.

Acceptance and joy at his son's change in outlook and return to his family came first**----not judgment and condemnation.** This is the model we should use for those who are experiencing intense feelings of guilt and shame. In the parable story, God is like the father, who wants to run after us **if we decide to change course.**

However, we need to repeat several things:

Acceptance does not mean approval of another person's past bad choices but it does recognize the need to engage with that person and acknowledge their pain. The hope is that acceptance by another person will act as the first step to move a person's thinking and feelings forward and away from shame so that healing can begin.

But, for this to work, the person who was feeling shame must have feelings of true remorse and seek genuine forgiveness.

Jesus himself, even on the cross, did not experience shame. He knew that he had done nothing that would cause him to feel shame. But **he certainly experienced intense humiliation**. The humiliation he felt was the result of actions by others-----stripping him naked, spitting on him, and then nailing him to the cross.

Why did he feel humiliation? Crucifixion was regarded as the most shameful and degrading death for a convicted felon----naked and stripped of all dignity, and nailed to a wooden post and exposed for all to see. He was spat upon, whipped, publicly cursed and jeered at, deserted by nearly all those close to him, and hung naked on the cross with all body parts exposed. What could be more humiliating than this?

But this is the same **Lord who offers us forgiveness** and **a clean slate** if we acknowledge our wrongdoing and the grief it caused to others and are serious about changing course. That is why we are told in the Bible that Jesus is the ideal person before God who intercedes on our behalf.

"For we do not have a high priest who is unable to sympathize with our weaknesses, ***but one who in every respect has been tempted as we are****, yet without sin.*

Let us then with confidence draw near to the throne of grace, that we may receive mercy and find grace to help in time of need. (Hebrews 4:15-16 ISV)

But because he did not give in to sin, he was able to bear **our** sins when he died on the cross, and can therefore offer us **amazing grace** in the form of **forgiveness and a fresh start** as a human being **with past wrongdoing removed and no longer remembered.**

And when we have confidence that God has forgiven us through the death of His son, then we can forgive ourselves and work at changing our thinking and the direction of our life even if we remain in prison.

In summary, there ***are*** positive things a person can do when overwhelmed by feelings of guilt and shame.

Questions to Think About

1. Are you able to ***feel remorse*** for the things you have done that greatly hurt other people including all the indirect victims of your crime? Do you have difficulty conveying to other people how badly you feel about things in your past?

2. Is there anyone whom you are able to trust and share your feelings with, so you could acknowledge how your thinking got badly messed up and how this led you to make bad choices that victimized other people?

Day 5 - Chapter 5: You *Can* Do Positive Things With Your Life Now While in Prison

In chapter 1, we reviewed why prison is such a negative experience (something you know all too well) and how all the negativity can be a barrier to doing or thinking anything positive. This problem is made worse by having to cope with feelings of guilt and shame, that we talked about in chapters 3 and 4.

In fact, after coming to prison, you may have moved through the various emotional stages of grieving that relate to any loss---for all the things you have lost or had to give up. These can be described in the prison context as follows: (From 'Five Stage of Incarceration, Prison Fellowship, https://www.prisonfellowship.org/resources/training-resources/in-prison/prison-culture/five-stages-of-incarceration)

Stage I: Denial - ***Denial*** begins when someone enters prison. It generally lasts between one and three years for those sentenced to a term of more than ten years. Some short-termers are in a state of denial for their entire sentence.

Those in the denial stage find it hard to believe they're really in prison. They focus on getting released. They tend to blame their situation on somebody else. Some prisoners work through denial gradually. Others leave this stage abruptly when faced with a crisis.

Stage II: Anger When a prisoner can no longer deny the reality of his situation, he often becomes angry with everyone. Some prisoners join prison gangs during the anger stage or get themselves covered with tattoos as a "f--k the world" protest.

Stage III: Bargaining Since no one answered his angry demands, a prisoner may resort to asking nicely for what he wants. Prisoners sometimes attempt to make deals with other people on the outside or inside. They promise they will mend their ways in exchange for the favor they seek. Or they may become religious and try to make a deal with God, to get them an early release.

Stage IV: Depression When it becomes clear that neither anger nor bargaining with others is working, depression often sets in. At this stage prisoners begin to face the consequences of their past actions and the current situation. They grieve the loss of freedom and the pain of separation from loved ones. Incarcerated fathers are devastated when they realize they won't be with their children perhaps until they are fully grown. Depressed prisoners often withdraw from family, friends, and even from other inmates.

Stage V: Acceptance Ultimately prisoners accept the fact that they are in prison for the long haul. This makes some prisoners emotionally numb to everything and everyone. Others go through a period of genuine soul searching. Some begin to accept responsibility for their situation and show a sincere desire to change their lives. This can take up to 12 or 13 years, until you are fully institutionalized and your only view of reality is prison.

Painful problems, like a family crisis or a move to a new facility, can trigger a return to earlier feelings. Prisoners must then work through the emotional stages of incarceration again so they don't remain in denial, anger, or depression.

Whatever stage in this process you are at in your incarceration, you still need to answer the question, ***"What can I do to make my life better given that I am going to be in prison for a long time?"***

What choices do you have?

Option #1 Do nothing different from what you did in the free world or that you're still doing now------showing constant resentment and overwhelming bitterness towards everyone and everything in your life. In other words, just continue with the same old negative dead-end thinking and the same old reacting like you may have been doing for some time.

Is this really what you want----more of the same? Is it leading to a happier and more fulfilling life? Is it doing you any good? Or, is it keeping you locked in the same depressing rut?

***Option #2* Put your time in prison to good use** by reflecting on your life to date, furthering your education, seeking to build relationships with other inmates who are not locked into all the negative aspects of prison culture and racial politics and being open to new ideas and thinking that may help make your life in prison better.

Being in prison does not have to be a waste. Many long-term prisoners have been able to expand their general knowledge, improve their physical health, and give up addictions that led them into trouble. These things all help to keep the "mental demons" at bay------depression and feelings of loneliness and worthlessness-----which are a fact of life for most long-term prisoners. Negative feelings do not need to dominate your existence.

Other Things You Can Do to Move Your Life in a More Positive Direction

1. **Develop a Productive Daily Routine** that may include a prison job and a daily physical work-out to help keep you occupied so time doesn't drag. It will also help you to

stay healthy and fit so you are more confident in dealing with challenges from other inmates.

Having a regular positive daily routine is good for your mental health, your sense of self-worth, and provides positive activities to fill part of your day. The more you can relate to the wider world beyond prison, the more you are able to put your life in some sort of context so that you come to see that prison isn't the sum total of all there is to your existence.

2. **Consider learning a skill or trade that might make you valuable to other prisoners** like sewing, repairing or making small electrical appliances, writing letters or legal requests for inmates that are nearly illiterate. This will help you gain respect from other inmates, pass the time during work hours and help you avoid dwelling on being in prison. It may also help give you a sense of self- worth----that you are contributing by performing a meaningful task and may even allow you to get a better prison job.

3. **Further your formal education** by working towards completing your GED. Or, if you have your GED, see if you can take some college courses or learn a trade in prison if this option is available to you.

   Furthering your education allows you to explore new ideas that can improve your life and make you feel more confident about yourself. It can help banish feelings of inferiority that you might have.

   Why should you continue to appear semi-literate, unskilled, or a drop-out simply because you weren't motivated in the past or didn't receive the encouragement to complete your education in the past? Most people inwardly respect those who appear more knowledgeable than themselves even when they may outwardly ridicule such knowledge.

Completing your GED or learning a skilled trade is an educational milestone that will contribute to your sense of self-respect and the respect of others. Why not reject once and for all the idea that you will always be a high school dropout? There's nothing glamorous about telling someone you weren't even able to finish high school.

4. **Participate in Workshops That Might be Applicable to Your Situation** like Anger Management, SNAP (Stop Now and Plan), or some Cognitive Therapy Sessions that might help you feel better about yourself and your life now.

5. **Consider corresponding with a pen pal to give you some contact in the free world,** not for "romance" (which rarely lasts, is usually artificial, can be manipulative, and often ends in disappointment), but to give you a chance to write about the things that concern you and interest you and provide you with an opportunity to ***improve your writing skills.***

   Also ***contact with a person in the outside world may reduce your sense of isolation.*** Most pen pals will at least treat you with respect, which is often in short supply in prison. Just be selective in who you correspond with. And recognize that most pen pal contacts will only remain for a few years at best and that they may drop you at any time without any explanation or chance for follow-up.

These are all things that can help ***your thinking and outlook.*** In so doing, you can become the better person, the valued human being you were meant to be---a person with a purpose in life, a person who wants to do the right thing, a person who can give to others rather than taking from others, and who sees that life is worth living, even in prison.

None of this is easy and you may be tempted to say "It won't happen to me", or, "I can't do this." But is that really the case?

Some other prisoners and prison staff may not want you to change your outlook and situation for the better. They may want you to remain stuck in the swamp of criminal thinking and mired in the racial politics of the prison subculture. But is that really what you want----the status quo?

Just because your life may look like it's been a dead-end up until now doesn't mean it has to stay that way. You do have some options. Let me illustrate this by telling a story.

I taught business subjects at a community college until I retired. I had a student who went to a party, had too many beers, jumped into the shallow end of a pool, and became paralyzed from the neck down.

He made a serious mistake and as a result he is stuck in the prison of his body that greatly restricts his freedom of movement. He can't move his arms or legs, he can't have normal sex, he can't do most things he could do before. At first, he wanted to give up and just die and he had a lot of anger to deal with.

But with help and encouragement from family and friends, he was able to move beyond this negative thinking and decided to make the best of his new situation. He actually went on to complete his college courses, build a career, and marry. He chose to make the most of his new restricted circumstances. Making a positive change in direction due to forced circumstances is possible.

That doesn't mean prison is in any sense a good place to be. It certainly isn't but it doesn't need to be all bad either. In summary, if you can further your education, expand your general knowledge through books, and build relationships with other inmates ***who aren't focused on the negative aspects of prison culture,*** then you can develop a positive sense of self-worth and community (because prison is a collection of people, good and bad, like any community).

Here is an account of what one prisoner serving life has written about his prison experience:

"I am 'institutionalized' because I literally feel ill when I am set-off by the Parole Board. Even though I am disappointed and frustrated, there is nothing I can do to change the outcome of their decision. Unlike many of my peers, I don't hate those who confined me, as I deserve the sentence as I was guilty of a serious violent felony---- the killing of a young man. Is there any measure of the worth of his life that I so heartlessly and maliciously ended?

But my sentence is that I would never be released. I have come to cherish the preciousness of the life I had taken; Woe is me, that to awaken to sense and responsibility, it took such a horrific act.

I came to accept through introspection, my sole responsibility for this act. Even though I pray I won't spend the rest of my life in this Texas Prison System, I know beyond a doubt, that it is I who was solely responsible for the consequences of that serious and final act.

Nevertheless, I cannot deny my humanness and need to get out to return to my family, and to know freedom again as a responsible productive citizen of my country. I am now aware and realize that I have a certain peace that overcomes the sense of frustration, despair and pain from the restrictions I have to put up with each day.

From the depths of my own adversity, I can hold up my head, and I can find within my thoughts positive and constructive things that encourage and strengthen me. It is because of my faith that despite sinking low due to my own devices and the resulting consequences, I can rise above it and I will go on. I can change. I do not have too, but I can and despite the odds against it caused by the system, I can make that change for the better.

Today I'm not the failure who entered this prison system that was statistically doomed to never be more than the killer that I was. Today I am drug-free, violence-free, and each day, I try to become a better person in some small way." -D. serving life in Texas (internet source for this written account is no longer traceable at time of publication)

Questions to Think About

The questions below are tough ones and there are no easy answers but I hope you will think about how you would answer them.

1. How does the prison environment work against any prisoner who tries to better himself by making positive changes in his education, his outlook, his thinking or his actions?

2. Can you list any things you have done since coming to prison to try to improve yourself? Possible examples completing your GED, taking courses, reading news magazines to keep up with things in the free world, attending self-help groups like AA or NA, or attending religious services.

3. Do you think you are basically a "good person" who just made a few mistakes and doesn't need to make serious changes in your thinking or in way you lived your life?

4. Are you currently satisfied with how you look at life (your current thinking), how you react to situations and people in prison (your current reactions)? Why or why not?

5. What things do you have to put up with ***over which you have little or no control,*** that make it difficult for you to cope in prison or to make real changes in your thinking or actions?

Part 2: Your Life *Can* Have Meaning and Purpose Now----in Prison!

In the chapters that follow in this part, we will explore what gives life meaning and purpose, and how that relates to your own situation.

This part deals with answers to questions about the meaning of human existence or "existential" questions.

The answers to these questions make up a person's view of the world, or what is called their "**worldview**".

Day 6 - Chapter 6: Is There Meaning and Purpose to Human Existence?

This is the most basic question about human existence. It is a question most people consider in some point in life. Let's explore this question about whether human existence has meaning and purpose ***for anyone.***

The basic question stated above leads to some other related questions that are often called "existential questions" because they relate to our existence. These include......

Why are we here on earth?

Is my existence just a random chance event or was I created by a Higher Being for a good purpose?

Pondering these basic "existential" questions brings other more personal questions to mind:

- Does anyone really care what I do or what happens to me, given my long incarceration?
- How do I make sense of my present existence and what I have to put up with day in, day out?

How we answer these questions is determined by whether we think human existence has any meaning and purpose ***for anyone.*** Are we just like ants in an ant hill going about our daily routine from birth until we die and disappear into oblivion, or is there a purpose to human existence----even in prison?

The answer to this question in turn depends on how we regard the existence of the universe including our own existence as thinking creatures called human beings. Did the universe and our existence come about by chance happening without any plan or purpose? Are human beings just another life form that came about by undirected random events? Are we simply part of a meaningless cycle of birth and death wherein we exist for seventy or so years and then face oblivion?

Or, is there is Higher Being who created the universe, is directing it on an ongoing basis, and who likely had a purpose in doing so? If such a Being exists (whom we call God), does His purpose include human beings like you and me? In other words, does this Higher Being we call God really exist?

If God doesn't really exist, then our life is meaningless. It has no purpose and it doesn't matter what we do with it. It makes no difference whether we are a saint or an unrepentant child molester. Why? Because if God doesn't exist, then there is no life after death and we answer to no Higher Being. Every person's existence will terminate in oblivion regardless of whether they led a good life or a bad life. If God doesn't exist, nothing we do really matters.

But if a Higher Being, a Super Mind and Power we call God----the Eternal Lord of the Universe----does exist, then the story is different. If He exists and brought this world into being, He must have had some reason for doing so. And if that reason includes us, then the whole picture changes.

So how would you answer the question, **"Does God exist?"**

The reason we need to talk about this question is because the answer we give forms the basis for what we might call our foundation beliefs or ***'worldview'***. And our foundation beliefs directly affect our thinking, and our thinking affects the choices we make in life ***and how we cope with bad things that happen in our life.***

Everyone agrees that God exists ***as an idea.*** But does He exist as a real personal being? There are really only two answers to this question.

1. God ***does exist*** as a real being. He created the universe including human beings and has revealed things to us about Himself and His purpose in creating the universe.

2. God ***does not exist*** as a real being. Instead, ***human beings came up with the idea of God*** in order to fill certain human needs. He is simply the figment of our imagination.

If we make the statement "God really does exist", we are expressing a statement of ***faith,*** not of ***fact.*** Why? Because there is no ***absolute*** proof that God exists. That is, God hasn't appeared to us personally and said, "See, I really do exist!"

Instead, we have ***reasons*** why we believe God exists and these reasons may provide proof to us beyond a reasonable doubt. But ***there is no absolute proof***, by which we mean proof without any possibility of doubt.

This isn't as bleak as it sounds, because ***neither is there absolute proof that God doesn't exist.*** To say God doesn't exist is also a statement of faith, not of fact. Neither the belief that God exists nor the belief that He doesn't exist can be proved or disproved in the absolute sense. What we do have are ***reasons*** supporting why God exists, reasons we find strong and convincing, reasons beyond a reasonable doubt. Likewise, atheists or agnostics also have reasons which convince them. So, is it simply a 50/50 draw as to whether God exists? Is that the best we can say?

This brings us to the ***concept of faith***, which we will discuss in greater depth in the next chapter.

Day 7 - Chapter 7: Every Person Puts Their Faith in Something

Every person has faith in something.

We couldn't run our lives without it. If a doctor operates on us, we have faith he knows what he is doing. If we cross the street when a signal says "walk", we have faith that the traffic signals are working in sync with the walk signal, and so on. If we are charged with a crime, we like to have faith that the justice system will treat us fairly. In prison, we may place our faith in other inmates or a prison gang to look out for us.

Christians and Jews put their faith in God based on some form of evidence that He exists. For example, for many of us, the beauty, order, and design of the natural world is proof enough to convince us of the existence of God as the great Designer of our world.

When we consider the complexity of the human body, the beauty and diversity of the animal and plant kingdoms, and the ***complex information*** in the DNA molecules that make up all living things, it is difficult for us to believe that all this resulted from random atoms colliding billions of years ago.

For me, this evidence of a Higher Intelligence or Super Mind operating in the universe is overwhelming and leads to the conclusion that an Intelligent Being we call God, was responsible for setting up our world. Yet I doubt many people believe in God only because they are convinced by ***thinking arguments*** that He exists.

If ***we don't want God in our thinking,*** we will come up with any argument we can to convince ourselves that He doesn't exist. ***Because if He doesn't exist, then we may feel we can live as if***

we don't answer to Him or anyone else and will do whatever we want, whether good or bad.

To be receptive to God, we also have to ***feel*** a need for him and most of us have that need because of our fragile human condition and weaknesses. All humans suffer in their life; all are sometimes lonely, depressed, or ill, and we all face the sure outlook of declining health as we age, and finally death.

In addition, most people seem to have a natural need to believe in something beyond themselves--what we might call the **spiritual need** we have as humans.

If we do **want** to believe in God, then He will give us the faith we need to do so. **God never rejects those who are open to Him, willing to learn about Him, and are interested in seeking after Him.**

So, it all comes down to what we want to put our faith in because **every person puts their faith in something**.

What do people who reject a belief in God put their faith in? They put their **faith in humanity** or the **institutions of humanity** to make a better world, like the environmental movement or the anti-globalization movement.

In prison, an inmate may decide, in addition, to put his faith in the protection and association offered by a ***prison gang***, so that he is with a group that respects him and with whom he can mix. (Unfortunately, this often comes at a steep price where the gang may demand things of him in return like absolute loyalty to gang orders to carry out assaults on other inmates.)

This may be a case of ***misplaced faith*** because human institutions sometimes do very harmful things and are very changeable. For example, the German people put their faith in Adolf Hitler but this ultimately brought nothing but misery, suffering, destruction of their country, and 16 million deaths of German citizens.

Most of the arguments raised against belief in the existence of God center around philosophical issues, such as the problem of pain and suffering and the existence of evil in the world. But none of these arguments are sufficient to disprove the existence of God. Therefore, it usually comes down to ***a matter of faith.***

Faith is a kind of knowing that does not rely only on reasoned-base proof (although proof based on reason is absolutely necessary since "blind faith" is worthless). But faith also has a characteristic that is more like intuition, or like when we say, "my experience tells me that such and such is true", or when we say "my gut" tells me something.

We are stating something we believe to be true **even though we cannot prove it with complete certainty. This is not an emotional response** but a response based on our knowledge and experience----what seems reasonable.

In fact, belief in God is like a wager, a staking of a claim of what we believe to be true. This idea was developed by a 17th century French mathematician, scientist, and inventor named Blaise Pascal. Part of Pascal's defense of Christianity has come to be known as ***Pascal's Wager***. It can be summarized as follows:

- Either God exists, or He doesn't.
- Which of the alternatives will you choose? Human reason alone cannot decide the matter for us ***with complete certainty***, so how will you choose? How will you place your bet, so to speak?
- You should bet on Christianity and a belief in God because if it is true, the rewards are infinite, while if it is false, your losses will be insignificant.

- Why? Because if it's true and you reject it, you've lost everything.
- But, if it's false, and you believed it, you've lost very little and at least you've likely led a good life.
- The best outcome then is to believe Christianity with its belief that God exists, and that it in fact turns out to be true.

The choice Pascal asks us to make on this issue is not simple or automatic. Many people, as Pascal noted, **avoid making a choice** and seek out other diversions where they can ignore the issue their whole life (including turning to alcohol, drugs, or the excitement of committing criminal acts). Others become indifferent, hoping that somehow, by luck, things will all turn out for the best.

Human-centered or "humanistic" views that deny the existence of God attract millions of people today, particularly among the so-called elites of our society. They follow the secular humanist worldview and share several things in common:

- They all have as their foundation belief, a faith in humanity;
- They all believe in the inner goodness of human beings;
- They believe all human beings will be good if given the proper laws, social environment, psychotherapy, etc.;

Based on the history of the last century in which human institutions and governments caused the deaths of millions of innocent people (under Hitler, Stalin, Idi Amin, Pol Pot, and others), it would appear this viewpoint also requires a great deal of faith---some would say misplaced or blind faith.

I believe there are far better reasons that compel us to put our faith in the other possibility-----that God exists, that we are God's creation, and that He promises good things for those who respond to Him and recognize Him as the Creator and Lord of the Universe.

When we decide in favor of a belief in God, we are declaring that certain things are true:

- That there is a power greater than ourselves, infinite and endless;
- That we and everything else in the material universe are the result of God's creative purpose and not the result of blind purposeless chance;
- That God is the ultimate thing that is real and that connects you and me to the rest of the created world;

If these things are true, it then follows that God is much greater than any human being and that He has ultimate control over any of His human creatures. This means He is the ultimate authority, the ultimate power, the ultimate judge, and the one who decides our final destiny.

Many people find this belief threatening to them. Why? Because it forces them to recognize **we are not the masters of our own fate** and **we can't simply do whatever we please without consequences**. We answer to the Higher Power we call God---the Eternal Lord of the Universe.

Many people do not want to recognize these things. They believe they answer only to themselves and can make their own rules of right and wrong.

Some prisoners even pride themselves on being rebels and outlaws from society who answer to· no one. This is a false view of reality that often leads to a wasted life in prison.

What does having faith in God do for us? Does it free us from the problems that go with being human? No. And it will not free us from prison. Nor will it make us instantly good, (but it should make us less bad).

But it does offer some real benefits, which when taken as a whole, can make a real difference in a person's life. So, what are these benefits of having faith in a Higher Being----someone greater than any human being?

1. Faith in a Higher Being, a personal God who cares about us, gives us a way to pick ourselves up when we make mistakes without being crushed by guilt, shame, and regret, because God makes it possible for us to be forgiven for our bad choices.

2. Faith in God helps us to feel we are never alone even if others including family and friends abandon us.

3. Faith in God provides us with a moral compass from a source that is greater than any human being so we can measure our actions and use it as a benchmark in guiding the choices we make. This in turn enables us to take responsibility for our mistakes and failures and make positive changes.

4. Faith in God provides us with a sense of purpose and mission in life since this Higher Being tells us He is interested in each of us, has a plan and purpose for each of us, and will reward us we seek after Him. We just have to start making Him an important part of our life.

5. Faith in a Higher Being gives us hope that there is something better planned for this earth and for each one of us, including the promise of a wonderful future existence after we die----if we seek it out.

6. Faith in God also makes it possible for us to connect with a wider faith community on the journey of life, to support and sustain us when we have needs, so we are not alone.

For these reasons, I believe Faith in God makes more sense, better reflects real life, offers true hope, makes the world a better place, and makes our individual lives work better.

Still, there have always been people who have no use for a Higher Being or no desire to believe in God or look into this further. That is their choice.

But, it may be something that could ***help give you*** a better outlook on your life and help you see that your life can have purpose and a positive future.

If you have little hope or see little purpose in your life right now, what have you got to lose by exploring this further?

Has the path your life has taken up until now made you feel good about yourself or your life to date, or given you peace of mind?

Has it made you value yourself as a human being or earned you the respect of others?

Is it really where you want to be in your thinking?

Here's a summary of **the implications** of the decision every person has to make whether to believe or not believe in the existence of a Higher Being we call God---the Eternal Lord of the Universe:

If there *isn't a* Higher Being we call God....	**If there *is* a Higher Beingwecall God...**
Then, there is no purpose in the universe or to human existence.	Then, there is likely a purpose to the universe and to human existence because human beings were given certain characteristics that relate us to the Higher Being we call God.
Whether you live another 50 years or die today makes no difference to anyone since no one will remember you for very long after you are gone, particularly if you spend a long time in prison. Your value a human being is very small.	Every human being has great value to God since each person was created in His image. As a result, He has a plan and purpose for every human being if they search it out and find it; but He won't force anyone to make Him a part of their life. We have freewill to seek after Him, to ignore Him, or rebel against Him.

Therefore***, it makes little difference on how you live your life***---whether you were a good person or a child molester or serial killer---- because all human existence ends in meaningless oblivion.	Therefore, it ***does*** matter what each human being does with his life---whether he tries to lead a good life or whether he chooses to rebel against God by ignoring Him or violating His moral laws like the Ten Commandments. Why? Because we answer to Him for the choices we make, whether good or bad.
Your life in prison can never have much meaning or purpose because your existence has no significance, meaning or purpose. It really makes no difference to anyone what you do with your life or how you behave in prison. You are alone and on your own. Once your family ignores you, no one really cares whether you exist or don't exist.	What you do with your life, while in prison ***is important to God because He has an interest in you.*** Since you have control over whether you choose to respond to Him or ignore Him, it does matter what you do with your life while in prison. He made you and He wants a good destiny for you but you have to include Him in your life.

How will you choose?

Chapter 8: Does a Higher Being Really Exist? If you say, No-----Do You Have a Good Answer for the Questions that Follow?

Does a Higher Being----the Eternal Lord of the Universe---who made and cares about His human creation really exist? If so, would you want to know about Him, particularly if He was personally interested in YOU----a member of that creation He brought into being?

As we discussed earlier, we can never have absolute proof that God exists. But, neither do we have absolute proof that God doesn't exist.

What we have instead are ***reasons*** to believe that there is a Mind and Power behind the universe that we call God. We are never asked to believe in this Higher Power and Mind on the basis of blind faith.

Belief in God ***is ultimately a choice each of us makes*** on the basis of the arguments for and against the existence of a good God.

Here are four questions to think about that may help you decide one way or the other. Ask yourself, "*Do I have good answers to these questions?*"

1. **Why does the universe exist rather than nothing at all?**

Science and atheism have no answer to this question. Science can explain what *is*, what exists, but cannot explain ***why*** it exists. Only the creator of something can explain why there is something rather than nothing.

A **Creative Mind** remains the only rational explanation for existence of the created universe. The less credible alternatives are that the created universe created itself out of nothing, or that it always existed.

2. **How did life and living things come about from non-living matter?**

   Science has no credible explanation how **life on Earth came about from non-life.** It is as mystified about the emergence of life from non-life as it is about the emergence of non-life from nothing.

3. **How do we explain human consciousness which is the ability to be self-aware of what is going on around us?**

Humans appear to be **the only beings in the universe that are self-aware.** How did **self-aware creatures** come into existence in a universe that is otherwise totally without self-awareness?

4. **Where did the Energy and Mind behind the Universe come from?**

The Dilemma -

To be an atheist is to believe that:

- The universe came into existence all by itself;
- Life and living things came from non-life all by itself;
- Human consciousness came about all by itself.

For me, the argument that there was a Creative Mind/Power who brought it about seems more reasonable. How many complex things do you know of that just come into being on their own?

What is more, the amazing complexity of our planet points to a deliberate Mind and Power who not only created our universe, but keeps it going with absolute precision. If not God, what or who is the Mind/Power behind this complexity?

5. **Why are there so many things about the Earth that are 'just right' for life?**

Let's review some of these 'just right' conditions for life.

- The size of the Earth is perfect for the amount of gravity needed to bind a thin layer of mostly nitrogen and oxygen gases to the Earth's surface, a layer that extends only about 50 miles above that surface. If Earth were smaller, the gravitational pull would be too small and such an atmosphere would be impossible, like the planet Mercury. If Earth were larger, its atmosphere would contain only free hydrogen, like Jupiter, making life impossible.

- **Earth** is the only known planet equipped ***with an atmosphere of the right mixture of gases to sustain plant, animal and human life***.

- The **Earth** is located the right distance from the sun. Consider the temperature swings we encounter, roughly -30F degrees to +120F degrees. If the Earth were any farther away from the sun, we would all freeze. Any closer and we would burn up.

- Even a very small change in the **Earth's position** to the sun would make life on Earth impossible. The Earth remains this perfect distance from the sun while it rotates around it at a speed of nearly 67,000 mph. It is also rotating on its axis, allowing the entire surface of the Earth to be properly warmed and cooled every day.

- Our **Moon** is the perfect size and distance from the Earth for its gravitational pull. The moon creates important ocean tides and movement so ocean waters do not stagnate, and yet our massive oceans are restrained from spilling over across the continents.

- **Water** is colorless, odorless and without taste, and yet no living thing can survive without it. Plants, animals and human beings consist mostly of water (about two thirds of the human body is water). You'll see why the characteristics of water are uniquely suited to life: It has wide margin between its boiling point and freezing point. Water allows us to live in an environment of fluctuating temperature changes, while keeping our bodies a steady 98.6 degrees.

- **Water** is a universal solvent. This property of water means that various chemicals, minerals and nutrients can be carried throughout our bodies and into the smallest blood vessels.

- **Water** is also chemically neutral. Without affecting the makeup of the substances it carries, water enables food, medicines and minerals to be absorbed and used by the body.

- **Water** has a unique surface tension. Water in plants can therefore flow upward against gravity, bringing life-giving water and nutrients to the top of even the tallest trees. This is why even sandy soils hold water so plants can survive. Also, water freezes from the top down and floats, so fish can live in the winter.

- Ninety-seven percent of the Earth's water is in the oceans. But on our Earth, **there is a system designed which removes salt from the water and then distributes that water throughout the globe.** Evaporation takes the ocean waters, leaving the salt, and forms clouds which are easily moved by the wind to disperse water over the land, for vegetation, animals and people. It is a system of purification and supply that sustains life on this planet, a system of recycled and reused water.

- **The human brain** simultaneously processes an amazing amount of information. Your brain takes in all the colors and objects you see, the temperature around you, the pressure of your feet against the floor, the sounds around you, even the dryness of your mouth. Your brain holds and processes all your emotions, thoughts and memories. At the same time your brain keeps track of the ongoing functions of your body like your breathing pattern, eyelid movement, hunger and movement of the muscles in your hands.
- The **human brain** processes more than a million messages a second. Your brain weighs the importance of all this data, filtering out the relatively unimportant. This screening function is what allows you to focus and operate effectively in your world. The brain functions differently than other organs. There is an intelligence to it, the ability to reason, to produce feelings, to dream and plan, to take action, and relate to other people.
- **The human eye** can distinguish among seven million colors. It has automatic focusing and handles an astounding 1.5 million messages simultaneously

Evolution focuses on mutations and changes within existing organisms. It does not explain the development stage of the eye or the brain, particularly when they are incomplete and not working properly or at all. A half-functioning eye or brain would be a real disadvantage and make an organism very vulnerable and unlikely to survive. If the eye or brain were created fully functional all at once, this would not be a problem.

In summary, do you have a good explanation for how all this has come about? Is blind chance the best and most reasonable explanation or is there a Super Mind, Intelligence and Power behind it all?

For me, it seems more reasonable to conclude that all these 'just right' conditions indicate that a purposeful Mind/Power Designer is behind it all.

What do you think?

Day 9 - Chapter 9: More Questions that Need Satisfying Answers: *Do You Have Good Answers for These Additional Questions?*

6. **The universe had a start or beginning. Who or What caused it to come into existence?**

Scientists are convinced that our universe began with one enormous explosion of energy and light, which we now call the **Big Bang. *This was the singular start to everything that exists*:** the beginning of the universe, the start of space, and even the initial start of time itself.

The universe has not always existed. It had a beginning. What caused it to come into existence? Scientists have no explanation for the sudden explosion of light and matter. Science cannot explain ***why*** it came into being-----only that it did.

7. **The universe operates by uniform laws of nature that we can set down in precise mathematical equations. Why? Where did these laws come from? Who brought them into being?**

Much of life may seem uncertain, but look at what we can count on day after day. For example, gravity remains consistent, a hot cup of coffee left on a counter will get cold, the earth rotates in the same 24 hours, and the speed of light doesn't change on earth or in galaxies far from us.

How is it that we can identify and formulate the laws of nature that never change into mathematical equations? Why is the universe so orderly, predictable and so reliable, so we can predict things like eclipses centuries in advance?

8. **The DNA code contains the information that programs a cell's behavior including the ability to make perfect copies of itself. Where did this information come from?**

Someone who writes an instruction manual does so with purpose. In every cell of our bodies ***there exists a very detailed instruction code,*** much like a miniature computer program.

As you may be aware, a computer program is made up of digital information, either ones and zeros, like this: 110010101011000. The way they are arranged tells the computer program what to do.

The DNA code in each of our cells is very similar. It's made up of four chemicals that scientists abbreviate using the letters A, T, G, and C. These are arranged in the human cell like this: CGTGTGACTCGCTCCTGAT and so on. There are three billion of these letters ***in every human cell***. The DNA coding is a three-billion-lettered program telling the cell how to act in a certain way. It is a detailed instruction manual built in to every human cell.

How did this very complex information program get encoded in each human cell. How did this complex coding originate? **Who or what did the coding?**

These are not just random chemical molecules but precise chemical molecules organized in a very detailed way to instruct each cell how a person's body should operate and reproduce itself.

Natural biological causes are completely lacking as an explanation for this programmed information in each living cell. You do not find precise coded information like this without someone intentionally constructing it.

9. **What is the Cause for the Existence of the Universe**?

Consider the following premises:

Premise 1: **Whatever begins to exist has a cause**.
Things do not suddenly pop into existence for no reason. Whatever begins to exist has a cause.

Premise 2: **The universe began to exist**.

Conclusion: Therefore, **the universe has a cause**.
Something or ***Someone*** caused it to come into existence.

Until the middle of the last century, it was widely believed the universe had always existed. However, since Hubble observed that the universe was expanding and the discovery in the 1960s of background radiation, it has become the overwhelming consensus of modern science that the universe began to exist, and did so with a Big Bang, some 13.7 billion years ago and space itself came into existence with the Big Bang.

As scientist Stephen Hawking and others have shown, not only matter but even time and space themselves came into existence with the Big Bang. That means that the Being or Thing that caused the universe to come into existence was outside of time, space and matter.

Furthermore, the precise fine-tuning of the universe, whose non-changing physical laws and constants were set at the first moments of the first second of the Big Bang, imply that such a cause was also unbelievably intelligent.

But there is something else. This First Cause acted deliberately and freely to bring about creation. It was not held back by any other force or power.

So, in summary, we are faced with a First Cause, a Mind/Power/ Intelligence who itself had no known cause (because it was outside of time, space, and matter), but was also changeless, powerful and intelligent, and who acted freely and deliberately.

What or who could that First Cause be?

This First Cause sounds a lot like the God of the Bible, a book which begins with the words, " *In the beginning, God created......*" In my view then, the most reasonable explanation for that First Cause of the Universe coming into being is the Mind/Power we call God, the Eternal Lord of the Universe.

10. **Where did concepts of good and evil, right and wrong, come from, given that these are basic moral concepts that are accepted by all societies everywhere?**

In an atheist world view, you have ***no objective basis*** to call anything ultimately good or evil.

Atheist morality is like the rules of a local dining club, where men must wear jackets and women must wear skirts. These are home-made, subjective human rules for the mutual benefit of members at a particular time, place, and culture. They are open for review at any point, depending on local demand.

Christians and Jews understand ***morality to flow directly from God's essential being***. God is a holy God - which means that He is good, He is love, He is just, He is merciful, He is faithful. What we call righteousness (or, "doing what is right") flows from these aspects of His character.

Without that ***objective basis for justice and goodness from the First Cause***---the Lord of the Universe----morality would be just a human invention that could change at any time. In such a world, there would be no ultimate justice and nothing would be right or wrong in itself.

But our whole system of law and ethics assumes there is an objective basis for what is "good" and what is "evil" that is higher than any human being. That is why criminal offenders are found guilty and sent to prison. People who believe in the Bible believe that actions are wrong if they violate the moral laws, like the Ten Commandments, that this Being gave us. That then is the standard for right and wrong, a moral standard from a source beyond any human being.

The argument can be framed as follows:

Premise 1: *If God doesn't exist, then moral values determining good and evil that are true for all people at all times and in all places--do not exist.*

Premise 2: *But human beings do accept that evil exists--- that actions such as rape, murder, and child molesting are regarded by all societies at all times as being evil and wrong.*

Conclusion: Since Premise 2 is true, then God must exist. Why?

Because **without God**----who is a higher source of authority than any human being and whose moral commands most humans accept---- **we have no objective basis for saying good or evil exist and are things we experience and all relate to.**

In summary, what do you think are the most reasonable answers to these questions----that they can best be answered by the operation of random chance or that they were brought into existence by a Super Mind/Power we call God?

Day 10 - Chapter 10: Has the Higher Being we call God---the Eternal Lord of the Universe---Communicated to Humans?

In the last chapters we discussed reasons for believing in a Higher Being we call God based on questions about our world and the universe that require answers. In this chapter, let's assume for now that such a God exists, and that He created the universe-----including human beings.

If this is the case, we could reasonably make a number of assumptions that result from that conclusion. For example, would it not be reasonable to assume that this Being ***had some purpose*** in bringing the universe and all that is in it into existence?

Would this purpose (at least as far as earth is concerned) not reasonably include humans, the ***only*** species of intelligent creatures capable of responding to this Being and appreciating the universe He created?

Is it not also reasonable that this Being would have wanted to **communicate to these humans information about both Himself and His purpose for bringing this universe into being**, particularly if His purpose was meant to include them? Without such communication, humans would know nothing about this Mind/Power that controls the universe.

Where would we look for such a communication? If it was to be effective it would have to have certain characteristics:

- It would have been around for a very long time so that it was ***available to people in many time periods up to the present.***

- It would need to ***be in a form that was both permanent and could be easily used and distributed***.
- It would ***need to claim to be a communication from this Higher Being***.
- It would be need to be ***readily available and widely distributed all over the world*** so that all peoples could have access to it and examine it.
- It would make the claim that it was from this Higher Being and that it conveyed His very thoughts and purpose.
- There would need to be some way to test the claims it makes in order to test whether they are valid.

Does such a communication medium in fact exist? Yes. Such a communication ***claims*** to exist in the book we call the **Bible**. It claims to be the communication of God that was transmitted through select human beings in the past and written down by them.

If this Higher Being had a particular interest in people, is it not reasonable that he might give them moral principles to show them how they should interact with one another and with Him in order to have a successful life, and then communicate these values to them?

This is the very claim the Bible makes. For example, the moral principles we call the ***Ten Commandments*** were given in the Bible so that human society can function in a civilized manner. It includes the commands, you shall not murder, you shall not steal, you shall not tell lies regarding your neighbor, etc.

In the next two chapters, we will explore in more detail what the Eternal Lord of the Universe has communicated to human beings.

Day 11 - Chapter 11: What Things Has the *Eternal Lord of the Universe*---Communicated to Humans?—Part 1

We have discussed how it was reasonable to conclude that a Higher Being, a super Mind/Power ***exists*** who created the universe and everything in it, including time and space, out of nothing and keeps it in running order.

In addition this Higher Being created one type of creature that was different from all other animals by giving it vastly superior mental and physical characteristics---characteristics that reflect in some ways what this Being Himself was like. In addition, we proposed that He had a purpose for doing this and would likely want to communicate with these beings who were "*made in His image*."

We considered what form such a communication might take from this Being to humans and why a written form would be the most likely. We then discussed whether any such written forms of communication claim to be from this Higher Being and why the Bible seems to best fit the bill.

Here is a list of some of the things this Being has communicated to human beings through the Bible:

1. There is **only one Supreme Being** who created the heavens and the earth and everything in them.

Isa 45:5-7 GWv I *am the LORD, and there is no other.* **There is no other God besides me.** *I am the LORD, and there is no other. I make light and create darkness. I make blessings and create disasters.* I, *the LORD, do all these things.*

2. **This Being made one species "in His own image"**, human beings----to be somewhat like Himself although on a much-

reduced scale, and to have the specific ability to rule over all other creatures. Here is what God said to the angels who assisted Him in the creative process......

Gen 1:26-27 GWv *Then God said, "Let us make humans in our image, in our likeness. Let them rule the fish in the sea, the birds in the sky, the domestic animals all over the earth, and all the animals that crawl on the earth."* So God created humans in his *image. In the image of God he created them. He created them male and female.*

3. **He is a Moral Being**

God is a Moral God and the source of all moral laws (like the Ten Commandments), and gave humans the ability to determine what is good and what is evil. To assist in this, he gave individuals a built-in **conscience** that works in part, even when people aren't familiar with God's moral laws.

Gen. 3: 22 GWv Then the LORD God said, *"The man has become like one of us, since **he knows good and evil**.*

However, He told them much more than this. He reveals many things about Himself in the Bible, particularly **things about His character.** What is He like? Let's go through the main attributes of Eternal One, Lord of the Universe and God of the Bible

4. **He is a God of Love**:

The main defining characteristic of the God of the Bible is that He is a God of love. In fact, He isn't just a God who *shows* love for humans, but the Bible says, God **is** Love.

1Jn 4:8 NLT *Anyone who does not love does not know God, because God is love.*

What does Love mean in the Biblical sense?

- Love in the Bible refers **to seeking and doing what is right, good, and helpful for another person**, or, seeking to do what is in the best interests of another person. It is not a feeling like romantic love.
- Love is the very opposite to planning or carrying out actions that are hurtful or that harm another person. These are often criminal acts committed against another person that include stealing, lying to, defrauding, raping, assaulting, or murdering another human being.
- God's love is shown to us by always seeking our highest good, **what is best for us in the long term,** even when He allows us to make bad choices in the short run. Allowing us to suffer is often the only way He can get our attention so we will consider making changes.

5. **He is a God of compassion, kindness and mercy**.

Many prisoners have never been shown much kindness or compassion in their lives and as a result, they have not shown much kindness or compassion to others in their life.

But this is not true of the God of the Bible. **He knows what we are like** ----weak, and subject to screw-ups. Here is what the Bible says about God's compassion, kindness and mercy:

Psa 103:8-14 GWv *The LORD is compassionate, merciful, patient, and always ready to forgive. He will not always accuse us of wrong or be angry with us forever.*

He has not treated us as we deserve for our sins or paid us back for our wrongs.

As high as the heavens are above the earth- that is how vast his mercy is toward those who fear him.

As far as the east is from the west- that is how far he has removed our rebellious acts from himself.

As a father has compassion for his children, so the LORD has compassion for those who fear him.

He certainly knows what we are made of. He bears in mind that we are dust.

6. **He is a Lawgiver**

In order to determine what is right and just and what is wrong and evil, He has given to humans, clear, simple, **basic moral laws of right and wrong---The Ten Commandments**---- so that we can have a successful lives and peaceful communities.

These moral laws are absolute----***true for all people in all places in all times***---- and include that you shall not steal, you shall not lie, you shall not murder, you shall not commit adultery, etc.

He holds us personally accountable if we break these laws since every human answers to Him for their actions.

7. **He is a God of Justice and Truth**

He is a God for all people, including victims of evil actions. Therefore, He promises ultimate justice to victims for the evil acts that other individuals commit.

However, He will show mercy to wrongdoers ***if*** they respond to Him by confessing their wrongdoing, **asking for forgiveness,** and by making a genuine effort to **change the direction of their lives**.

Sadly, because many people including many prison inmates look only at the judging side of this God and not the forgiveness and support side, they reject a belief in this God. God gave us basic moral laws "for our good" so that individuals, communities, and society at large would function well.

If a person, community, or society chooses not to follow these laws, the result is much more likely to lead to insecure, unhappy lives that are destructive for our partners, our families, all those who care about us, and also harmful to our communities and society at large.

Just as the Lord of the Universe gave us physical laws like the law of gravity, He also gave us moral laws. If we choose to ignore the law of gravity and jump off a cliff, we will face serious consequences.

Why would it be any different if we choose to ignore and rebel against His moral laws? Rebelling against Him or repeatedly violating His moral laws has negative consequences.

What is more, He makes it plain that He will reward those who seek to keep His commandments but will cause the **permanent destruction** unrepentant wrongdoers who choose to rebel against Him and leave Him out of their lives. That is what His justice is all about.

Here is what the Bible says about those who repeatedly choose to rebel against His laws, have no interest in changing their ways and are completely unrepentant:

Psa 37:9 GWv ***Evildoers will be cut off*** *from their inheritance, but those who wait with hope for the LORD will inherit the land.*

In a little while ***a wicked person will vanish****. Then you can carefully examine where he was, but* ***there will be no trace of him.***

Psa 37:28 GWv *The LORD loves justice, and he will not abandon his godly ones. They will be kept safe forever, but* ***the descendants of wicked people will be cut off.***

Psa 27:38 GWv ***But rebels will be completely destroyed****. The future of wicked people will be cut off.*

8. He has also revealed why humans think bad thoughts, do bad things, often screw up relationships with other people, and **why evil, suffering, and death exist in the world.** We will deal with this aspect in a later chapter.

9. Lastly, He reveals that He Had A **Good Purpose in Creating Humans.** But He didn't leave things there. He then goes on to *reveal* that He had a **good plan and purpose in creating the Earth---**a plan that includes every human being ***if*** they choose to respond to Him. We will discuss that plan and purpose in much more detail in subsequent chapters.

Day 12 - Chapter 12: What Things Has God, the *Eternal Lord of the Universe*--- Communicated to Humans—Part 2?

We ended the last chapter by reviewing how the Eternal Lord of the Universe has a plan and a purpose for human beings that he has communicated to them in the Bible. He declares in the Bible that He formed the Earth for a particular purpose---***to be inhabited.***

Isaiah 45:18 GWv *The LORD created the heavens . God formed the earth and made it. He set it up. He did not create it to be empty but formed it to be inhabited. This is what the LORD says: I am the* LORD, *and there is no other.*

His ultimate aim is to fill the Earth with his glory ***through human beings.*** He said, in Num 14:21 KJv, *But as truly as I live, all the earth shall be filled with the glory of the* LORD. This will be done in the Kingdom of God in a renewed Earth under the rule of Jesus Christ, the King of Kings.

This is the subject matter of the gospel, which we will discuss in future chapters. The gospel is not about playing a harp in Heaven. ***It is about being an immortal being in a real world-wide Kingdom here on a renewed Earth***----more about this in later chapters. That is why in the Lord's Prayer, it says, "***Thy Kingdom come***, Thy will be done ***on Earth***."

We have already discussed how God said to the heavenly messengers (angels), "*Let us make man in our image, after our likeness.*" To be in the image of something, is like seeing your face in mirror---the image the mirror reflects back on your real face. Likewise, when God made humans "in God himself-reflecting his image", this means that humans were meant to reflect in our lives what God is like.

Reflecting God in our lives is what the Bible calls *"giving glory to God"*. To glorify something means to make it look great. So for God to say that He made us in His image is the same as saying that He made so **we could display** many of the things about Himself-----His character, His righteous laws for having a good life, and His creative genius---- **all so that He could share a part of His greatness with us.**

When we enjoy a beautiful sunset, or scene in nature, we are indirectly giving glory to God who made these things. The same goes when we are create something beautiful like a painting or write a great song or piece of music, we should also be giving Him glory because He is the ultimate "creator" and has passed on part of His creative ability to humans.

But we also give God glory when we follow His laws so that we can have a good life (particularly by following the Ten Commandments) or when we show kindness, compassion, mercy etc. to other people, or when we do something good for our neighbor.

This is because we are reflecting back to Him the things that are great about His character **in our own actions**, and that pleases Him.

Likewise, when we do things that are harmful to other people, this distresses **Him because we are turning away and rebelling against Him** by violating His laws like the Ten Commandments.

In fact, the second purpose God had in mind in creating the Earth and the Universe was to seek out a group of human beings from all of humanity ***who would voluntarily reflect back His glory***.

That is, the Bible reveals to us that He is taking out from all nations people **to whom He can give His Name**---which means

He regards them as members of His family. In the book of Acts 15:14 (GWv) we read:

"Symeon [Peter] has shown how in the first place God chose a people from among the nations who ***should bear his name."***

If you have been given another person's last name, you are considered part of their family. If we were to "bear God's name"---**it means we would be regarded as part of His family**.

In later chapters of this book, we will deal with His plan and purpose for the Earth and His plan and purpose for every human being who responds to Him.

In summary, here is a list of the main things that God-the Eternal One, Lord of the Universe-has revealed to us in the Bible:

1. His plan and Purpose for human beings and for this Earth;
2. A Moral Code to act as a compass for us to live by in order to have a happy fulfilling life and a peaceful orderly society as set down in the **Ten Commandments;**
3. An explanation of the ***reason for*** human screw-ups, evil actions, suffering and death;
4. The ***remedy for*** personal screw-ups, evil actions, sin and death that is also part of the Gospel message;
5. Personal histories of real people during the 1500- year period when the Bible was written explaining their screw-ups and how some were able to turn their lives around and find acceptance again with the Eternal One--- even after very bad actions like rape and murder.

In the next few chapters we are going to discuss what God has revealed to us about why ALL human beings screw-up, think bad thoughts, do bad things, suffer, and finally, die.

Day 13 - Chapter 13: Do We Really Need A Higher Being to Give Us Moral Principles about what is Right and Wrong? Why can't we decide for ourselves?

In the last two chapters, we discussed that one of the things God gave humans was **a basic moral code** so that both individuals and society could function without being dominated by evil actions and fear.

But many people in our society today reject such a God outright because **they don't want to be bound by any moral laws or have to answer to a Higher Being when they break those laws**. Many people want to be completely free of such a God.

Others argue that we no longer need a Higher Being as the source of our basic moral principles. They regard such thinking as old-fashioned and superstitious and that we have moved beyond the concept of wrongdoing as "sin"----an offence against God.

Instead, many say we are now in an age where a person can do anything he wants, subject only to the laws of the land and his own judgment. This is true in the sense that all people have free will to make their own moral choices.

And this thinking certainly fits well with the ***strong streak in our human nature that resists authority*** or anything we think infringes on keeping us from doing what we want.

Our human nature even prompts us to reason that ***if we deny that God exists, then His moral laws won't exist for us and the concept of "sin" will have no meaning for us.***

We will have no need for God, religion or to be "saved" because there will be nothing we need to be saved from. (Of course, that still leaves us with the problem of ongoing suffering, declining health, and ultimately, death.)

What then do we use to guide our moral choices? How do we decide one action is "good" and another action is "bad". What do we use as our compass or yardstick?

Is it simply a matter of our ***feelings*** or intuition? Or is there a yardstick provided by society? If so, what is that yardstick based on?

In fact, we can go back a few steps and ask, "If God doesn't exist and if He didn't give us basic principles of right and wrong, as we discussed earlier, then ***where did the basic concepts of morality come from?*** If not from God, ***who invented these principles and how did others come to accept them***?"

In other words, ***what is the source of authority to tell us what is right and wrong?***

Some would say the source is within you and is reflected in ***the feelings and intuition of individuals,*** or collectively, of ***human society***. Should this make us feel good? I don't think so. Let's look at why this is a problem on two levels: at the individual level and for society at large.

While every person is capable of much good, ***we are all very good at rationalizing our actions and failures-- even when they hurt others***. In addition, each of us is so wrapped up in our own selfish wants and needs that our view of life's issues is subject to our own ***feelings of the moment***, which are very changeable.

Our wants and needs are driven by our own self-centeredness, self-interest and sense of self-preservation. For example, a hard-core criminal thinker may say to himself......"I *will lie, cheat, assault, steal, rape, or even murder-----if it gets me what I want or need.*"

In the absence of a standard of right and wrong from a Higher Being, we will usually choose what we *feel* is in our own self-interest. After all, isn't what **I** think and feel just as good as what anyone else thinks and feels?

So, how could people ever get agreement on what is right and wrong----what we call the **morality** of a given action? How could society decide that murder is wrong if each person could each make their own rules of right and wrong?

If the focus is simply on **me and what I feel right now**, this can cause a person to override and ignore what his conscience is telling him because **feelings are often the stronger influence on what we choose to do**. We may do the right thing today because it **feels** like the right thing to just now, but **what if it feels entirely different tomorrow** in a different situation or with different people? Our own conscience is often not enough to get us to make the best choice.

If each of us simply made our own rules based on ***how we feel at a given point in time***, then society could soon break down into total anarchy where robbery, rape, murder, became the norm.

Why? Because our actions would reflect our feelings and self-interest at the time. We would constantly be saying to ourself, **"**I *will do what feels right for me just* NOW."

Most prisoners are perfectly aware of this type of thinking because it is the way to survive in prison. But would it be desirable for society to operate on this 'law of the jungle' basis?

The central point is this: **If there is no God, no ultimate, unchanging authority for moral behavior, then who is to say that theft, murder, rape or robbery are wrong?**

The only questions then from those who commit such acts are, "Why not?", 'What's to stop me?" or, "Give me a good reason why I shouldn't do these things."

We could probably agree that allowing every person to determine his own rules of right and wrong would not be a very good solution if we wanted a peaceful society with people living in harmony with one another.

However, what if groups of people came together and agreed upon rules of right and wrong? Wouldn't this solve the problem of coming up with moral standards without a need for God? Isn't that what happens in a democracy when individual citizens vote in governments to pass laws for the good of society?

Yes, it is, but there is still one serious problem with this approach. **Different societies make different rules and all societies change their thinking over time.**

For example, Adolf Hitler was elected by the German people in the 1930's to improve German society. One of the means he undertook to do this was through the extermination of so-called "inferior races", disabled people, and some criminals, etc.

Without an ultimate external authority with absolute standards of right and wrong, who is to say his actions were wrong? After all, he was elected by the collective will of the German people.

If each individual is his own moral judge and the only measure of right and wrong are the laws passed by governments elected by society, then ***on this basis***, the laws passed by Hitler's government to exterminate whole populations ***were perfectly moral.***

In fact, this is what Nazi war criminals claimed, who were put on trial at the war's end. They said they were morally bound to follow the laws of the elected government because **this was the**

highest authority they recognized. They did not recognize a source of moral law from a Higher Being.

This is perfectly reasonable if there is no higher unchanging authority which we can appeal to for deciding right from wrong.

However, nothing is permanent regarding right and wrong in the laws passed by government. The laws that governments pass are just a reflection of the will of the people in a society **at a point in time**. But the will of the people is subject to change because the thinking of society changes over time.

What is regarded as morally wrong today might well be morally acceptable tomorrow. Look at the changes we have witnessed in the last 50 years regarding society's attitudes towards divorce, adultery, homosexuality and abortion, to name a few. Fifty years ago "society" condemned these things based on the laws of the time; now these things are legally allowed and accepted.

In fact, the wide acceptance of a universally-recognized moral code------the Ten Commandments—is an argument for the existence of God---a Higher Being- --who communicated a basic moral code to his human creatures.

So, we need to ask, "Could people really live in harmony in society if we didn't have a Higher Being who set the foundation rules concerning right and wrong **for all human beings for all times and places** ?"

It all depends on your point of reference. If we don't have an ultimate unchanging respected authority that resides *above any human being or human institution as a reference point, an authority that is the source of principles of right and wrong that are true for all time, and for all people*------ **then we will feel free to change, ignore or violate any rule if it suits us.**

Is it not reasonable then, to conclude that **there is a definite need for a universal unchanging moral code from a Higher Being,** *a Being that was far greater than any human, that holds each person accountable for his actions; a Higher Being that people would respect as the source of rules for what is right and what is wrong?*

It is hard to imagine the well-being of any society being served by people setting up their own individual codes of morality and making their own rules that simply reflect their own feelings, desires, and self-interest at a given point in time.

And it is hard to imagine a stable, universally-accepted code of morality coming from humanity at large. For example, countries today can't even agree on what should be included in basic human rights as defined by the United Nations Organization.

And if society doesn't function well without everyone agreeing to follow some basic rules of right and wrong from a recognized Higher Being, is it not reasonable that individuals likewise will not thrive without attempting to follow these same principles?

Questions to Think About

1. Do you think both society and individuals are better served if there is an accepted moral standard like the Ten Commandments that is widely recognized and regarded as being from a source greater than any human being? Why or Why not?

2. Do you personally recognize the Ten Commandments as a God-given source of moral laws? Why or why not?

3. Did the existence of God-given moral laws like '*You shall not steal*", '*You shall not kill*", have any significant

influence on your decision to commit criminal acts in the past? Why or why not?

4. Do you feel any differently today now that you are in prison and have had time to reflect on things in your past?

Day 14 Chapter 14 : Other 'Life Principles' God Has Given Us to Have a Better Life

In the last chapter, we discussed our need for a recognized authority that is greater than any human----to give us an unchanging moral code as a guide for us to make good moral choices in our life, choices that will result in stable human relationships and peaceful thriving communities.

We believe that such a moral code was given to us by the Eternal Lord of the Universe, in the Bible.

But since God made humans "in His image" and wants human beings to have thriving relationships, He has also given us some **Life Principles that will guide us in our human relationships-**--particularly those between a man and a woman. These principles are designed to provide the greatest happiness and stability in human relationships, given that we all have sin-prone fallen natures. So here are three of these principles:

Life Principle #1: **God is not a respecter of persons** and He clearly states that **all human beings are all of "one blood"** so that there is only **one race---the human race**.

Acts 17:26 *And* ***hath made of one blood all nations of men*** *for to dwell on all the face of the earth, and hath determined the times before appointed, and the bounds of their habitation;*

Acts 10:34-35 *Then Peter opened his mouth, and said, Of a truth I perceive that God is* ***no respecter of persons: But in every nation he that feareth him, and worketh righteousness, is accepted with him.***

Gal_6:10 As *we have therefore opportunity,* ***let us do good unto all men****, especially unto them who are of the household of faith.*

Importance: This principle teaches us not to discriminate against other human beings on the basis of race or ethnic background---because God doesn't---but should be respectful of all people, attempt to live at peace with them, and do good when we encounter them. This is the fulfillment of the second great command to ***love your neighbor as yourself.***

Life Principle #2: Because God is no respecter of persons, **He is open to all people and seeks a relationship with every single person-----regardless of their current circumstances.**

We make a relationship with God by seeking Him out so we can know about Him. This includes talking with Him in prayer, asking Him to help us in facing life's challenges, and asking Him for forgiveness for our screwups and failures.

This is what the first great commandment is all about: ***to Love God with all our heart, soul and mind***.

He wants every individual to seek Him out: As it says in Isa 55:6-7 GWv, *Seek the LORD while he may be found. Call on him while he is near. Let wicked people abandon their ways. Let evil people abandon their thoughts.* ***Let them return to the LORD, and he will show compassion to them. Let them return to our God, because he will freely forgive them.***

Importance: This principle teaches us that **God is interested in each of us and wants each of us to include Him in our life every day.** If we are willing to do that, He will show us compassion by forgiving us for our bad deeds and providing us with a hope-filled future.

God also recognizes that human relationships are very important----particularly intimate ones involving sex. Therefore, He set up a model for human relationships that would result in the best outcomes for men and women in a sin-prone world. This brings us to Principle #3.

Life Principle #3: God's Plan for Human Relationships is based on what He designed and therefore what works best---what we might call the Biblical Model for Human Relationships. It is based on the following concepts:

1. **There are two biological sexes, male and female.**

Gen 1:27 GWv So *God created humans in his image. In the image of God he created them. He created them male and female.*

Importance: For stability and greatest happiness in life, our gender identity should match as closely as possible with our biological sex.

2. **Ideally, a man should leave his birth family and start his own family by seeking a female partner with whom he wants to share his life.** They should then formally marry and become 'one flesh' in a mutual loving relationship

Gen 2:24 NLT *This explains why a man leaves his father and mother and is joined to his wife, and the two are united into one.*

Importance: While this is not an easy task these days---to *find a suitable mate who wants to share their life with you*----this is **the model that God set up** to best bring about the greatest human happiness and a stable thriving society.

Marriage **encourages a man to accept responsibility** and start a family **in return for support, companionship, love, and satisfying his sexual needs.**

It's not a perfect arrangement---some marriages are unhappy and end in divorce----but research consistently shows that

men thrive best when they are in a stable married relationship of one man and one woman.

For example, men's sexual urges are much better satisfied in a stable marriage relationship because married men have far more sex than unattached men. Also, they live longer, have fewer health issues, have much lower criminal involvement, much lower suicide rates, and so on. And a married relationship is also the most stable structure for raising happy, thriving children.

In summary, if we are willing to accept the model that the Eternal Lord of the Universe gave us in the Bible, then we have a much greater chance of having a happier, more fulfilling life That is there is a good chance that our life may become better for us. We can do so at any time and in any circumstance.

Day 15 - Chapter 15: From Belief in a 'Higher Power' to Belief in the God of the Bible---the *Eternal Lord of the Universe*

Let us accept for now that it is more reasonable to explain the things we discussed in the last few chapters as having their origin in a Supernatural Mind and Power we call God--the Eternal Lord of the Universe. That is, let's assume that the existence of such a Being is the best explanation to account for :

- The existence of "something" (i.e., the universe} rather than "nothing";
- How life and living things came from non-life;
- Where all the complexity and evidence of design in the natural world came from;
- The origin of human consciousness and the ability of human beings to be self- aware;
- The beginning of the universe---the thing that caused it to come into existence and why;
- The origin of very precise laws of physics that regulate the universe in a predictable way and that keep it from collapsing on itself;
- The origin of the complex information in the DNA molecules in each living cell that regulates all living things and allows them to reproduce exact copies of themselves;
- The origin of moral concepts of good and evil that are universally accepted.

> The next logical question is this: If such a Being exists and did all this magnificent creative work, would it not seem reasonable to assume that this Supernatural Mind/ Power also ***had some purpose in bringing this all about?*** Otherwise, why bother at all? After all, when humans create something, there is almost always some purpose in mind.

Also, If this Mind/Power went to the trouble of bringing into existence one set of creatures—human beings---who function on a much higher level than all other animals with much greater physical, mental, emotional and spiritual capabilities----is it not likely that He had some special purpose in creating them since ***they are they only creatures that can respond to Him in some way?***

And if He had some purpose in making them with superior capabilities and with an understanding of right and wrong, it is ***reasonuble to conclude that He must have wanted to communicate with them in some way*** so they could interact with Him, learn about His purpose in creating them in the first place, and provide them with some guidance on how to live their lives.

What would likely be the best way to do this?

This would depend on whether He wanted robot-like creatures or whether He wanted to give them the ability to make their own choices--what we call "free will". Robots don't give much pleasure because all their responses are pre-programmed, but creatures with free will can respond voluntarily (like a dog to its master).

So if this Mind/Power opted for giving these superior creatures free will, then He would not want to be directing their every step. Rather **He would likely want to be in the background so as to not interfere with their free will choices**. This would rule out direct contact with his human creatures except in rare exceptional circumstances.

We have already discussed what form of communication would probably work best if this was the case. It would be ***some form of written communication*** since He gave humans the ability to both speak and to write in languages. In addition, a ***written form of communication*** such as a book has many advantages:

- It is a more or less permanent record of what He wanted to communicate with them;
- It is portable and could be carried by people wherever they went;
- It could be translated into multiple languages so it could be read by people all over the Earth.

In the last few chapters, we made the case as to why it is more reasonable to believe that the universe, living things, and human beings were brought into existence by the Eternal Lord of the Universe, rather than believing it all has come about by pure chance.

However, we now want to take this one step further and make the case that this same Higher Being has revealed Himself to humans in a form of written communication we call the Bible.

In fact, this Higher Being makes the following claims in the Bible:

1. **That He created the universe** and all that is in it including time, space, and matter out of nothing. That is, **He is the 'first cause' of all that exists.**

The very first verse in the Bible declares.......

Gen 1:1 ***In the beginning God*** *created the heaven and the earth.*

The God of the Bible then clearly **claims to be the First Cause-----the originator of the universe and all that is in it**. This also means that if He is the source of everything in Nature, then He is greater than Nature, rather than being a part of nature.

2. **That He made one form of living things-----namely human beings-----in His own image---**beings that were more complex than all other living things and that have characteristics more like this Higher Being.

In speaking to the angels, who carry out his creative work, He said......

Gen 1:26 KJV *And God said, Let us make man in our image, after our likeness: and let them have dominion over the fish of the sea, and over the fowl of the air, and over the cattle, and over all the earth, and over every creeping thing that creepeth upon the earth.*

Gen 1:27 *So God created man in his own image, in the image of God created he him; male and female created he them.*

This tells us that human beings were to have some of the characteristics that only God possessed but that were not possessed by any other creatures. These include:

- A higher form of intelligence and consciousness compared to any other creatures so that **they have dominance over the earth and over all other animal creatures**. For this reason, human beings are not just another animal because ***they alone were created in the image of God.***

- A unique **ability among all created things to make moral choices by being able to determine right actions from wrong actions.** In addition, God revealed only to humans **His moral laws**, and gave ***only*** them **a conscience** to help guide their moral choices.

- **An ability to communicate in both spoken and written speech using language.** While some animals like dolphins may be able to communicate by making sounds, none but humans have the ability to communicate using written speech.

- **An ability to have a religious/spiritual sense**----a sense of wonder about the universe and a desire to explore it, a desire to reflect on why we are here, and to seek after a Higher Being for information about the meaning of our existence and our ultimate destiny.

- While animals rely on instinct, **humans are conscious beings** and can express feelings such as love, and ***form relationships*** with other people and with God Himself.

- Human consciousness also gives humans a unique ability (unlike any other living creatures) to **appreciate art and beauty.**

Given these characteristics that the Higher Being chose to bestow on His human creatures, itseems reasonable that He would have an interest in communicating with them in order to have a relationship with them.

Would He not wish to convey to them....

- **His desire to have a relationship with them and then inform them about the nature of the relationship He seeks with them?**

- **The reason why He created them----the reason for and meaning of their existence?**

- **The good purpose and final destiny He wants for them?**

There are various religious books but **only one claims to be the very words of the Lord of the Universe**---and that book is **the Bible.** Over 800 times the Bible claims it is recording the very words and thoughts of God himself.

In addition, **the Bible alone claims that this Higher Being can accurately predict the future** and He has given predictions in the Bible about specific events many years before they happened (**called "prophecies"**) that subsequently came to pass with amazing accuracy.

This is because God exists ***outside of time and space***--which He created in the first place. Therefore, the past, the present and the future are all the same to Him.

This is quite different from human prophets down through history like Nostradamus, who claimed to be able to prophesy about the future. Most such prophecies are vague and very general rather than specific like Bible prophccies.

In addition, the Bible makes claims that agree with what we know about the universe or have experienced. These examples tell us that the Bible reflects the world as it really is----what is observed scientifically or what we have observe personally. Here are some examples. This should give us confidence that we can trust what is in the Bible.

What we Observe or Experience	What the Bible Claims
We observe order and design in the natural world ----evidence of a Super Mind and Master Designer.	The Bible claims that God created the heavens and the earth and everything in them. It was not the result of blind chance.

Scientists have confirmed that the universe had a beginning.	The Bible claims "*In the beginning God created...*" God is the first cause and brought the universe into existence.
One species of animal, human beings, are far superior to all other living things and have vastly superior physical and mental capabilities.	The Bible claims that God made one species of animal "*in His own image*"---that is, somewhat like Himself, although on a much lower level. Gen 1 :26 GWv says, *Then God said, "Let us make humans in our image, in our likeness.*
Only humans can exercise control over all other living things and over their environment. No other living things are able to do this to the same extent.	The Bible claims that God gave humans the specific ability to rule over all other creatures: Gen 1:26-27 *Let them rule the fish in the sea, the birds in the sky, the domestic animals all over the earth, and all the animals that crawl on the earth." So God created humans in his image.*

Human beings alone of all living things have a **moral sense**-----the ability to determine what is right and wrong.	The Bible claims that God is the source of morality and gave human beings the ability to know what is "good and what is evil." Gen. 3: 22 GWv *Then the LORD God said, "The man has become like one of us, since he knows good and evil.*
Humans alone have a conscience that helps them distinguish between actions that are right and good and actions that are wrong or evil.	The Bible claims that God gave human beings a built-in conscience that works in part, even when a person isn't very familiar with God's moral laws. Rom 2:14-*15* NLT *Even Gentiles, who do not have God's written law, show that they know his law when they instinctively obey it, even without having heard it...**for their own conscience and thoughts either accuse them or tell them they are doing right.***

Part 3: Moving Beyond a Bitter Existence of Regret and Exploring Another Way

Day 16 - Chapter 16: Why Do People Commit Crimes and Other Bad Actions? Why is there Evil in the world?

All people think bad thoughts that may get converted into bad actions. It is a common feature of the human condition that leads to feelings of guilt, failed relationships, dysfunctional families, and failed dreams. Those who commit criminal acts are just following through with ***more serious forms of the same condition that affects all human beings.***

Why is this so? Why do even the best people mess up sometimes and do things they greatly regret? What is the source within human beings that brings thoughts into our minds that give rise to bad deeds that we later regret?

The world is divided in its understanding of why we do bad things. For most people, bad thoughts stay as bad thoughts and go no further, or result in actions that may hurt others but which are not criminal offences (for example, bullying another person). For convicted felons, these bad thoughts get converted into bad deeds that violate the criminal code and are called crimes.

If we understand the ***root cause*** why these bad thoughts arise and why they get converted into bad deeds, particularly criminal bad deeds, then it is possible to consider making changes in our thinking so that this doesn't happen.

None of us can really make meaningful changes in our thinking or outlook on life if we don't recognize that **we all have a problem and need to be able to recognize the source of that problem**. That is why this chapter may be the most important chapter in this whole book, because how we understand the root cause of bad behavior and its remedy----***depends on how a person views human nature.***

There are basically two "worldviews" of human nature that explain why bad thoughts come into our mind and why we may act on them to do bad things:

1. The Judeo-Christian (Biblical) View

2. The Secular Humanist View

In this chapter, we are going to explore the Judeo-Christian view of human nature because the Bible is very blunt and straightforward as to why human beings "screw up". It states the problem clearly in the first few chapters of the Bible.

The Judeo-Christian View of Human Nature

The Judeo-Christian or Biblical View of Human Nature is based on a number of assumptions:

- That there is an Eternal Being we call God that is the first cause of all things that we know or we experience. This Being created the universe and everything in it. His final act of creation involved human beings.

- The first human beings, Adam and Eve, were unique among all creation in that ***they alone were created in the image of this Eternal Being***. This meant they possessed features that other creatures lacked: they stood upright; they had hands to use as tools to shape their environment; they possessed reason, self-awareness and the ability to think and make their own choices, that is, to choose their own destiny.

- Unlike other creatures who relied on instinct, these first humans interacted with the Eternal Being and they were lords of the earth, ruling over all nature, including their own human nature, and caring for the environment.

- At first things went very well. Everything was in perfect order because the Eternal Being Himself ruled through these first human beings, who were His willing agents.

- However, the Eternal Being gave them free will to choose their own destiny. If they decided to tell the Eternal Being to get out of their lives, He would agree.

- If they chose to be free from this Being, they would be free to direct their own lives but would no longer be under this Being's direct care, guidance and direction. They would be on their own.

- To make sure they could use their free will, this Being gave them **one command**: ***they were not to eat of the fruit of one particular tree in the paradise where they lived***. This tree was ***the tree of knowledge of good and evil***. So, they had a choice to make.

- At first, they followed what the Eternal Being asked of them but then one day, they chose what ***they*** wanted to do rather than what the Eternal Being asked them to do----***they decided to make their own rules of what was right and wrong***. This choice was expressed by violating the one command that God gave them-----eating of the fruit of the tree of knowledge of good and evil.

As a result of their choice, they violated the command of the Eternal Being. As a consequence, ***sin was introduced into the world*** because they chose to not obey the one rule that God had imposed on them. They rejected the Eternal Being and ***turned to themselves as the final authority of right and wrong.*** In making this choice, they committed the first sin.

Sin is choosing to do what you know is illegal, wrong, or forbidden.

When sin was introduced into the world, things dramatically changed for the first human beings:

- God got out of their lives, but in so doing, they suddenly lacked the power and wisdom to exercise ***proper control*** over nature or over their own thoughts and actions.
- In fact, they were expelled from the paradise where they had lived and entered a world that was now distorted and out of balance: storms, earthquakes, and natural disasters could no longer be prevented; the ground was cursed so that it no longer yielded abundantly to the plow; instead, weeds, rot, rust, disease-causing bacteria and parasites infested everything; animals that lived in harmony with them now fled from them or would turn on humans in fear and hunger or would eat and destroy their crops.
- Pain, suffering, and death became permanent features of the environment.
- What is more, ***at the personal level, human nature was seriously affected***. The harmony that Adam and Eve enjoyed with one another was destroyed; the loving, caring relationship they had both with one another and with the Eternal Being was poisoned because they could no longer control their own natures.
- Selfishness, pride, greed, and lust entered their world, causing strife, misunderstandings, and heartbreak that contaminated even their most intimate relationships.

  This act of rebellion resulted in a change in the nature of these first humans so that ***they now had a natural attraction towards choosing to do evil***.

This tendency was passed on to all their descendants so that it resides in each human being from birth. It is part of our human nature which takes the form of evil thoughts and actions which lead to ***choosing self (what we know is wrong) over choosing what God wants.*** This is the meaning of **sin**.

This **rebellion** against God and His moral laws has thrown the entire creation out of joint and everything is distorted by sin. For example, a seemingly good thing like art can become distorted by sin and turn into pornography, which is an evil expression of art; intimate physical love became lust and a desire to dominate or rape another.

As a result, **the relationship of the Eternal Being with the first humans was broken and they became separated from Him.** In addition, He no longer communicated with them face to face. He was gone from their lives.

These effects **we all inherit as human beings**. In our natural state, we suffer, we deteriorate and we ultimately die; we do bad things that distort our relationships with one another and we are separated from the Eternal Being.

The penalty for sin is death. That is why all humans die so that without some change in this situation, we are in a state that the Bible describes as ***"without hope and without God in the world".*** (Eph 2:12)

This then is the main reason why all human beings screw up and why there is evil in the world. **We all have a natural desire to choose what is evil and we all commit sins. No one is exempt**.

Fortunately, God also offers a way of dealing with our sin problem. So, **choosing evil is not inevitable**. Instead, we can choose to seek after God by acknowledging our sin problem to

Him, and receiving His remedy (which we discuss more fully in later chapters).

This then is the Judeo-Christian view as to why people screw up and why there is evil in the world.

However, there is another view as to why people screw up and do bad things that harm others in their families or communities. It is called the **Secular Humanist** view. It is the opposite of the Biblical view. The best way to explain this view is to compare it with the Biblical Viewpoint given to human beings by the Lord of the Universe.

Let's look at a comparison of the two contrasting worldviews of Human Nature and how it impacts on offenders----the Biblical or Judeo-Christian view and the Secular Humanist view.

Contrasting Worldviews of Human Nature

Biblical View	**Secular Humanist View**
Human beings have a built-in tendency to choose evil right from birth---- but ***bad choices are not inevitable*** if a person is raised in a family that teaches them about right and wrong and if the community supports and enforces these concepts of right and wrong.	**Human beings are basically good right from birth.** They are ***corrupted by things in society, things outside of themselves-----***not because of their own thinking and actions.

A person makes bad choices because of their ***built-in human tendency to choose evil.*** It comes from ***within the person.***	A person makes bad choices because ***of things in society***----poverty, racism, bullying, lack of opportunity, discrimination ----things that are ***outside the person.***
Every human being has free-will to make good or bad choices. Therefore, each person is responsible for their actions and will ***answer to a Higher Being for the evil they do to others.***	***Human beings do not have freewill.*** The choices they make are the result of the environment in which they were raised and their genetic makeup-----**things over which they have no control**.
Jesus Christ makes forgiveness and redemption possible for any human being----***if we repent of our bad choices and resolve to make changes.*** So, the God of the Bible gives us both ***freewill*** but also ***a way out*** seeking and receiving forgiveness.	There is no such thing as forgiveness for past screw-ups from a Higher Being. Moving beyond bad choices that harmed others is difficult or impossible although psychotherapy, or anti-psychotic drugs can sometimes help.

You have control over your thinking and are held **primarily** responsible for your actions.* However, there is a remedy to help you move beyond past bad actions----- the choice to repent, seek forgiveness from God, and move your life in a different direction. This is also something you have control over.	***You are not primarily responsible for your bad choices (since they are mainly due to chemical reactions in your brain.* A prison doctor or psychologist*** backed by the authority of the state will decide how to fix your tendency for making bad choices. You will have little or no say in the matter.

(* This author recognizes and fully accepts that some forms of mental illness are caused by a chemical imbalance where treatment with drugs or therapy is totally appropriate. In such situations, a person may have reduced responsibility for their role in crimes or bad actions.)

So, which of these two viewpoints do you think better reflects reality? Which view do you prefer?-----one that holds you responsible for your actions ***but gives you control for any changes you want to make?*** Or, a view that says you are not responsible for your actions, but leaves how to "treat" you completely in the hands of prison authorities and gives you little or no control or no say?

If you choose the Biblical view, God doesn't leave you in a hopeless position. He provides a way for us to deal with our past bad choices that provides hope for our future------no matter how bad our past screw-ups. That is where we are headed in subsequent chapters.

Day 17 - Chapter 17: How Valid is the Secular View of Human Nature?

The foundation principle behind the Secular or Human-centered View of Human Nature is that human beings are ***basically good.*** That is, that "being good" is the natural and default state for human beings.

But how valid is the thinking behind this---the concept that people are basically good and can be made even better when government authorities have control to make everyone in their image?

First and foremost, in my opinion, **anyone who rejects the wisdom of the Bible on this issue----*that human beings are not naturally "good" but prone to choose evil*-----** is rejecting what we find in the world as we really experience it.

Writer and commentator Dennis Prager dealt with this issue in some depth in his book, Genesis, God Creation and Destruction, in an essay entitled, "The Belief People are Basically Good is Foolish and Dangerous[1]." In this essay, he asked these questions:

"Are there any parents who haven't had to teach their children to be good people? How many times has the average parent told his or her child, "Say, 'Thank you' "? If people were basically good by nature, wouldn't telling a child once or twice suffice? Why would all of us need to be told thousands of times to express gratitude to someone who has done us a kindness?" (Prager, Dennis, Genesis, God Creation and Destruction, Regnery Faith, Washington, 2019, pp 109-110))

He then lists some reasons why many people including those in government, the media and public education have chosen to believe the secular view that man is basically good? He states,

"... many people who don't believe in God and religion have to believe in man or they will have nothing to believe in---and that would lead to complete despair". (Ibid, p 111)

"Another reason is the rejection of the Bible as people's primary source of wisdom. Bible-based Jews and Christians do not believe people are basically good because the Bible says they're not." (Ibid, p111)

Prager also discusses a third reason which is that most people in America (and by extension, much of the Western world) live in societies that are prosperous and peaceful where even the vulnerable are looked after. Therefore, there is a perception that countries like the USA are populated by good, decent people, and this is largely true. But Prager then states,

"And America's decency is largely the legacy of its adherence to a biblical worldview throughout most of its history." (Ibid, p.111)

However, I would add, this has not been the norm either for the world at large, either historically over time or currently from a geographical perspective, and it is true of only of a minority of countries. Instead, chaos and disorder are the norm.

Prager also lists the implications that flow from adopting this false ***secular view of human nature, that people are basically good.*** I have summarized his reasons as follows:

1. Children are not taught to be good. That is, parents may not feel the same need to teach children how to be good if they believe that goodness comes naturally. Prager states, "Only when people realize how difficult it is to be a good person do they realize how important it is to teach goodness." (Ibid, p112)

2. God and religion will become morally unnecessary. Prager asks, "If we are basically good, who needs a transcendent source of morality...?

   He then adds, "...the more people have come to believe people are basically good, the less religious and the less Bible-centered they have become. And the less religious and less Bible-centered they have become, the more they have come to believe people are basically good". (Ibid,112)

So, what are the implications of moving away from the Bible-centered view of human nature that Prager outlines? I would suggest that over time, the concept of sin becomes irrelevant. A person may accept they made a bad choice or made a mistake, **but the idea that they sinned against a Higher Being is increasingly *rejected*.**

And once people reject the concept of sin and that they answer to a Higher Being for their actions, they are unlikely to believe we need forgiveness or salvation. As a result, **they may have little or no interest in seeking after God or including Him in their lives.**

The third reason Prager cites as to why the idea that people are basically good is dangerous is this: Society, not the individual, is blamed for evil. He says, "If people are basically good, the reasoning goes, the evil that people do must be caused by something outside of them. Why else would a basically good creature commit evil? This is why the most widespread modern explanation for violent crime has been poverty. 'Poverty causes crime,' the argument goes." (Ibid, p112-113)

But then he adds, "But this is just not so. For one thing, the great majority of poor people do not commit violent crimes. They don't because they have a moral value system that tells them criminal violence is wrong. And what could possibly link poverty to, let us say, rape? If one argues poor people steal because of poverty, at least there is plausible link between the two. But what has poverty to do with rape." (Ibid p.113)

Despite what Prager argues here, I recognize that the environment in which a young person is raised has a great influence on their values and outlook on life, but it is rarely the whole explanation for criminal actions.

But when the majority of people come to believe that evil actions are primarily caused by things in society that are separate from the person, then, as Prager points out, people who think this way tend to strongly support more government programs to solve the problems of evil and dysfunction in society.

This is not what the Bible teaches is the solution to the problem of evil. Jesus made this very plain in his teaching. Regarding the source of evil, he said, *For from the heart come evil thoughts, murder, adultery, all sexual immorality, theft, lying, and slander.* (Mat 15:19)

Jesus makes no mention of things outside the person like poverty or racism. He blames evil actions for coming right from the human heart,

The Bible then teaches **that the problem of evil is rooted in each person himself---with his thinking**, and stresses the need for each individual to take responsibility for wrongdoing by making changes to his thinking. In particular this means he needs to **adopt better moral values as part of his thinking** and **exercise more self-control over his actions**.

As Prager points out, those that hold to the secular view of human nature tend to encourage people to do battle with problems in society rather than stressing **the need for people**

to reform their own moral outlook as a way to exercise more self-control.

Prager summarizes by saying,

> "Values and moral self-control matter far more than outside forces. Nearly all people who commit violent crimes do so because they possess a malfunctioning conscience, a morally defective value system, and/or lack impulse control." (Ibid, p114)

He then gives his prescription for making good people. He says,

"The best way to make good people is through the combination of good values, good laws, and a God who commands goodness----such as that of the Bible." (Ibid, p.114)

These are things the Bible clearly teaches. We can expand on them in more detail as follows:

1. **The need to teach children God-given moral laws like the Ten *Commandments* from a young age** in order to promote good moral values.

   The Bible says in Proverbs 22:6, *Train up a child in the way he should go: and when he is old, he will not depart from it.*

   Many prison inmates may never have been exposed to good moral training when they were children. This is not their fault but it may have got them off to a bad start in life. Fortunately, a person can change his moral thinking and adopt good values at any time in his life.

2. The need to emphasize, particularly in the home, as Prager points out, **that our main fight is not between**

each person and society. Instead, he says, "...the battle for a moral world is waged primarily through the inner battle that each of us must wage against our nature: against weakness, addiction, selfishness, ingratitude, laziness, and evil." (Ibid, p. 115)

3. Also, **good moral examples in a child's life** are necessary for children to use as a model for their own behavior. If these are missing, it much more likely a young person will fall into criminal behavior.

   The ideal situation is described in the Bible as follows: (Mal 2:15 NLT version) *Didn't the LORD make you one with your wife? In body and spirit you are his. And what does he want?* ***Godly children from your union****. So guard your heart; remain loyal to the wife of your youth.*

   Sadly, many men in prison never had good fathers to guide them when they were growing up even though the Bible clearly tells us how important it is for young males to have a father who gives them both instruction in good morals, provides a good example for them to follow, and who gives sons appropriate discipline.

   In Eph 6:4, we read, *Fathers, do not provoke your children to anger by the way you treat them. Rather, bring them up with the discipline and instruction that comes from the Lord.*

4. It is also necessary that in order to produce good people, that parents teach their children **a healthy fear and respect for a good God who demands goodness from all human beings and to whom we answer for our choices**

However, people who believe that human beings are basically good may have no interest in the concepts of sin, the need for repentance, belief in a God who judges us for our moral choices, and hence of our need for salvation. This in turn cuts them off from other comforting religious concepts that reduce anxiety such as.......

•**Belief in a loving God** who is interested in each and every person and has a plan of salvation through the saving work of our Lord Jesus Christ that compensates for the failings of our corrupt human nature. This includes **forgiveness** from a loving God for our past mistakes----***which can greatly improve our mental health and give us a new sense of self-worth as a valuable human being.***

- Belief in a loving **God who is control of the Universe** including planet Earth and is overseeing things happening on this Earth, like climate change and other trends which create anxiety in so many people today. **This belief reduces our anxiety about the trends we observe and encourages us to be thankful, grateful human beings**.
- Belief in a loving God who **has a good plan for people here on a re-generated peaceful Earth**-----when wars, famine, and all the evils plaguing human beings will be suppressed and finally eliminated, in the coming Kingdom of God. **This belief gives us hope for the future.**

We will discuss all these things in greater detail in later chapters.

Day 18 - Chapter 18: Moving Beyond Our Screw-ups So We Are Not Dragged Down by Feelings of Regret and Despair

When the first human couple rejected the one moral command the Eternal Lord of the Universe asked them to follow, very bad consequences were the result. As we discussed a few chapters back this included a curse on human beings so that they would struggle and face hardship, they would have a tendency to choose evil, their health would decline over time, and finally, they would die. They were removed from the Garden of Eden. All creation and all their descendants were affected by this. The "very good" state of the creation no longer existed.

Fortunately for us, this was not what the Eternal Being had in mind as the ultimate outcome for His creation. God immediately ***promised the banished couple that He would one day send a descendant of theirs who would make things right for humans.*** It was a consequence of giving people free will----the ability to make choices. In addition, He gave each person a conscience to help them make good choices despite their tendency to choose evil.

However, we have all been given a conscience to counter balance this tendency to do evil but it has to be developed. This needs to be done from an early age by being raised with good family examples and being taught moral standards like the Ten Commandments. Only then will our conscience be effective and act for us as a built-in mental policeman to get us to reject bad actions. Most psychologists say this development must be in place by age 9.

In fact, when there are no counterbalancing influences in our environment, this tendency to make bad choices may come to dominate our thinking and we may go into a downward spiral of wrongdoing. This state of things is like being born with a handicap.

So, without this moral training, it will "harden" us to what is good both in ourselves, and others. Since we have no control over how we were raised or what moral principles our parents taught us or showed us by examples, **our later bad actions may not be *primarily our fault*** because we had no control over our early upbringing.

It is the natural attraction for evil within us (which we call our flawed 'human nature') that makes us susceptible to becoming involved in criminal activity. Why? Because it makes us blind to anything except our own selfish desires------what we want to do. As a result, ***our flawed human nature is the root cause of the bad choices we make.*** It is ***something every human being has to contend with***.

Not one of us is free from its effects---not you, not me. The tendency of our nature to do evil and the counterbalancing pull of our conscience to do good, means that we are constantly having to make moral choices. We ***can choose*** to do evil or to do what is right and good.

Because we have the free will to make these choices, we are held accountable for our actions by the system of criminal justice and by God.

While our family environment, our early upbringing and training, and our genetic make-up do ***influence*** the choices we make, ***they do not control those choices***. This is why Western society holds criminal offenders personally accountable through the criminal justice system.

Does this mean human beings are by nature evil? No!----only that they have ***a natural tendency to choose what is evil***. Evil only comes to dominate a person's life and hardens them to all that is good **if there are no counterbalancing influences pulling them in the other direction towards what is right and good**. One of the main problems with prison is that there are few other prisoners or influences pulling a person towards what is good. Prisons are dominated by criminal thinking (which we will discuss more in a later chapter).

In fact, evil is often defined as "*the absence of good*" which is probably a description of the reality of most prisons. And much of this negative thinking develops because of the way prisoners are treated. Some see no point in trying to better themselves and give up by leading a 'bad ass' existence of ongoing destructive behavior.

And every person gives in to sin----repeatedly---not just people convicted of committing crimes. This built-in tendency to sin is a problem that never leaves us as long as we are alive. It is part and parcel of being human and it is what hurts our relationship with God.

That is why, from God's perspective, ***we are all in need of transformation***. The personal transformation of each person is the solution to the problem of sin and its ultimate effect----death. We will discuss exactly what this means in later chapters.

In contrast to this, the ***secular approach to explaining why people do bad things*** relies on "experts" like psychologists and sociologists. They have all kinds of theories----like poverty, racism, and lack of educational or job opportunities. The problem is that no two experts agree on the causes they come up with and these causes don't apply across the board (unlike the Bible's explanation). For example, the overwhelming majority of children that grow up in poverty do not go on to become criminals. And some children from good stable homes with two parents go on to commit crimes.

In summary, only the Bible provides an answer for bad thinking and bad actions that affect every person and provides a way out.

Questions to Think About

1. What degree of influence do you think you had over the choices you made when you decided to commit the crime that landed you in prison? Do you think you are primarily responsible for the choices you made or is someone or something else primarily responsible? Who or what is that person or thing?

2. When you think about the crimes you have committed, how significant was the pull of your conscience before you decided to commit the crimes? Was it much of a factor? If not, why do you think your conscience had little effect on your choice?

3. Do you think the Judeo-Christian view of human nature reflects actual reality or is it unreasonable? If unreasonable, what do you think would be a more reasonable explanation of what human nature is like?

4. Why do you think people choose to commit criminal acts that they know will harm others? Do you think that deep down, they recognize such actions are wrong?

5. Do you feel you were given good moral and religious training and good examples as a child so that your conscience was a significant force in your decisions in life? If not, what do you think was missing? What would you change about your thinking if you could live your life over again?

6. If you had your own children, how would try to influence their thinking so that they would not follow in your footsteps and end up in prison?

7. If there is an Eternal Being who is the source of good and who wants us to attempt to reflect His ways in our actions, do you think He would be satisfied that you are trying to follow His ways in your current thinking and actions, or do you think He would regard you primarily as a person who is wholly given over to criminal thinking and criminal actions? Why or why not?

8. Do you think God would be justified in abandoning a person who was completely given over to criminal thinking and had zero interest in trying to change his criminal thinking and criminal life-style either in or out of prison? Why or why not?

9. Do you ever think He has given up on you or is about ready to do so? If yes, why do you feel helpless to change this? Have you given up on Him?

10. Do you ever feel you have given up on yourself by feeling that you have made too many bad choices so that it is too late to change your thinking and actions now?

Day 19 - Chapter 19: Gaining Wisdom Instead of 'Butting Heads'

A few chapters back, we discussed whether society needs an unchanging moral framework like the Ten Commandments in place that the community respects, tries to practice and enforce, or whether society is better to make up the rules as it goes along and change the moral rules as feelings change.

Most would agree that the Bible provides such a set of widely accepted moral laws that are based not on what other people think, but ***on a source that is greater than humans***----the Eternal Lord of the Universe. That is why courts of law ask you to swear on the Bible to tell the truth when you are called to testify. It is regarded as a source of recognized moral truth greater than any single human being.

But what if we reject the idea of God-given moral laws for regulating society? What is the alternative? Would a world free of basic laws like "*you shall not murder, you shall not steal, you shall not lie, etc.*" and without the means of enforcing them, make for a happier, freer community for people?

I don't think so. Without some basic moral concepts like the Ten Commandments---that everyone accepted---our world would soon descend into anarchy and the law of the jungle. Likewise, only when a person lives as God intended-----***within the moral structures He gave us for our own wellbeing***-----can a person have a good, fulfilling life or can a community feel truly free.

It has been observed that when human beings abandon God-given laws or God-given social structures like traditional morality or the family unit, the result is not greater freedom and happiness but greater problems for society. This is the opposite to doing what is wise.

When people abandon the self-control that is encouraged by the moral laws of the Bible, then the state is often called upon to intervene or to enact coercive laws backed up by law enforcement and the criminal justice system in order to preserve peaceful, safe communities.

When this happens, restrictive laws like curfews are passed by legislatures, more police enforcement is required, and communities feel less safe.

Most people hope that others in their community will follow moral rules like the Ten Commandments so they can make wise choices that work for the good of all----for the offender, his family, and his community. **This is what having wisdom is all about.**

Wisdom is about making good choices that promote the happiness and well-being of both ourselves and those around us, including a partner, family and friends. We "get wisdom" ***when we learn to live in harmony with God's laws*** rather than ignoring them or rebelling against them.

Wisdom isn't about simply following rules but ***trying to do the right thing in the way we live and making good choices for the benefit of both ourself and those we care about*****----**our families, or friends and our community.

When this becomes our mental outlook and way of thinking, then we come to see God's moral laws more ***like a compass*** or ***reference point to help guide us through the unknown.*** When we do this, wisdom starts developing on its own, because we are making wise choices.

So, to be wise is to understand and accept the world as it really is----a world organized by a loving God who gave us rules to guide us in making our free will choices. If we accept our need to be guided by these rules, then there is a far greater chance that we will make wise choices and have a successful life

Most of us have a natural tendency to want to violate rules at some point. But choosing to repeatedly violate God's moral rules means we will pay a steep price, particularly in terms of our long-term happiness and well-being.

When we examine what is happening in society today what do we see? When people disregard God's laws, we seem to see more family problems and marital breakdowns, more messed-up kids, more mental problems, more laws restricting our freedom, more social problems, more crime, more prisons, longer sentences and these things (particularly the last two items listed) only make matters worse as problems are passed on from one generation to the next.

The inevitable consequence is that society in general and individuals in particular will bump up against reality and against each other in painful ways.

At the personal level, being an outlaw or rebel against society ***isn't worth the steep price that has to be paid.***

So, the greatest problem each of us faces is not with our family or what society or the judicial system has done or not done to us. Deep down we all know that society isn't the primary cause of our problems (although it is often a contributing factor). Rather, it is **our own thinking and choices**.

When we recognize this, we can take charge and begin to make changes so that we no longer ignore or reject the principles that make for a happy and fulfilling life. This is true for every person including those who face many more years of living in prison.

Each of us has the power to make changes in our attitude and thinking so that we don't constantly butt heads with other prisoners, with our family, with the criminal justice system, with prison staff, and ultimately, with God Himself.

Even the concept of freedom isn't just about leaving prison. It's also about control over our thinking and our state of mind-----about facing up to the truth about the world as it really is **and then making wise choices.**

Also, human beings also have a natural instinct to seek or recognize something higher than themselves----what is usually called a spiritual or religious sense.

These two aspects of our human nature often ***pull us in opposite directions***. What we want to do is often in conflict with what we sense God wants us to do as reflected in our conscience.

We will likely have much better success in moving our life in a positive direction and developing wisdom, **if we base it on a foundation belief in the existence of the God of the Bible---the Eternal Lord of the Universe** and **try to follow His moral commandments.**

He cares about each of one of us. That is why He gave us basic moral principles to help us make wise choices and have a successful life.

Recognition of this Higher Being in our life is also the approach of groups such as AA and NA which have a good track record in helping people cope with addictions.

Such a belief also tells us we are never alone in our struggles.

However, before we move onto that more positive alternative, I would like to talk about the crime problem in society and how the thinking patterns of many **repeat offenders** are different from of the rest of the population. This type of thinking may not apply to your situation but you probably know other prisoners who appear to have this type of thinking.

Day 20 Chapter 20: Why Do People Commit Crimes That Harm Others?

There has been a problem with crime ever since people began living in communities.

A minority in every group of people engage in theft, robbery, fraud, kidnapping, rape, murder and other crimes. Because criminal acts harm individuals and disrupt the peace and security of a community, criminals are pursued, apprehended, tried in courts of law, and punished.

But the reason ***why*** some people commit crimes and others don't has perplexed those who make laws and those who try to understand human behavior for hundreds if not thousands of years. No society has ever been able to eradicate crime. Every society has a minority who chooses to violate the rules that society generally agrees to live by.

The age-old question then is, "*Why do some people commit crimes and do* so *repeatedly despite severe penalties or attempts at rehabilitation?*"

At root, it seems that **Criminal Behavior is caused by a person deliberately choosing to commit acts that are illegal or forbidden-----**actions they know are wrong,

This is the final conclusion of one of the most extensive studies ever undertaken on the causes of crime (a landmark work entitled, Crime and Human Nature, published by Harvard professors James Q. Wilson and Richard Herrnstein in 1986). Here are some the findings they highlighted in their book:

They found virtually no link between crime and poverty, racism, or oppressions;

- They did however find a strong link between crime and the lack of good moral training (which was often also linked to bad family upbringing and the influence of peer pressure);
- Their overall conclusion was that crime primarily involves a person making a **moral decision**---the choice by criminal offenders to commit crimes and break the law. Hence, persons who engage in criminal activities do so primarily because that is what they want to do;
- While a person's conscience typically tells them that criminal activities are morally wrong and not to go there, they override what their conscience tells them;
- They do know right from wrong-----but they deliberately choose to do what they know is wrong. Their choice is ***to do what they feel like doing***-----breaking the law or doing what is "forbidden".

In that sense, it can be said that ***choosing to commit a criminal act is a form of rebellion,*** not just against the community, but, ultimately, against God because He gave us moral laws like the Ten Commandments so we could have a peaceful orderly society.

When a person violates one of the Ten Commandments, in the religious sense it is called **Sin,** because it results in a violation of the moral commands given to us by the Eternal Lord of the Universe. The choice to commit criminal acts almost always leads, in the long run, to bad outcomes for the offender, families and communities, because all are harmed by criminal acts.

We all have to make choices every day on all kinds of things and future choices don't have to be the same as past choices. Future choices can be quite different from past choices, as our thinking matures based on our experiences and new information.

That is why there is positive hope for every person's future, regardless of their current circumstances.

Day 21 – Chapter 21: Why Is 'Criminal Thinking' Like Living Under a Curse?

In the last chapter, we discussed the problem of crime and how its cause is rooted in our flawed human nature. If a criminal act is a one-time occurrence for a person, then it is easier for that person to move on in a positive way even though they still need forgiveness, healing and restoration.

However, when a person ***repeatedly*** commits criminal acts, it can become a way of life and **the dominant form of their thinking-**----what is called **Criminal Thinking**. When criminal thinking sets in, a person's life may become defined by repeated criminal acts and repeated terms of incarceration.

This why it is like living under a curse, because 'criminal thinking' leads to repeated terms in prison where you have a relatively deprived unfulfilled life.

That is, when criminal thinking takes over a person's thinking, a life of constant rebellion outside the law may become inevitable. Some criminal offenders are proud of this "outlaw" existence. However, it is a total violation of what God intended when He gave us the law ***to love our neighbor the way we love ourselves.***

But the question still remains: why does only a minority of the population choose to make criminal choices, and why do some do this repeatedly?

In the last thirty-five years, researchers have established that many ***repeat offenders*** typically think differently from the rest of the population. Their ***thinking patterns*** lead them to constantly make irresponsible choices to commit crimes and often to also abuse alcohol and drugs. That is why I have called it a kind of 'curse', because it leads to so many bad outcomes.

The rest of the population may ***think*** about committing criminal acts from time to time, but built-in constraints on their thinking cause them to pull back and act responsibly.

Their conscience kicks in and tells them the crime they are considering is morally wrong and will be damaging to themselves, their families and their community. They also recognize that engaging in criminal activity goes against all the accepted norms of their families and community. Hence, the majority reject committing crimes even when there is an opportunity to do so, and most reject repeatedly abusing drugs or alcohol.

There is some evidence that family background may play a part. For example, some studies have shown that if one of your parents was a convicted felon, you have a much greater chance of also being a criminal offender, even if you were adopted and raised by a completely different family in a "*good*" family environment. This seems to imply there may be some biological or genetic link to criminal behavior although no "criminal gene" has ever been isolated.

While a person's level of schooling, lack of a father in the house (for males), poverty, drug or alcohol abuse in the family, and peer pressure may affect the likelihood you will commit a crime, these things do not in themselves explain why some individuals choose to commit crimes and others raised in the same environment do not.

Many kids are raised in poor, dysfunctional families where alcohol, drugs, and physical abuse exist, but most such children do not become criminals. In fact, some criminals come from stable families where there was moral and religious training and no substance abuse.

There is also evidence that many people who commit crimes have mental health conditions like ADHD or PTSD so that they act impulsively and do not have the built-in thinking **constraints** that allow most people to reflect on a situation before they act. These same individuals may turn to drugs or alcohol as a form of "self-medication" in order to get relief from the symptoms of ADHD or other sensory conditions.

Still, **there is nothing that makes it inevitable that a person will engage in criminal activity** on the basis of their family background or the environment in which they grew up. But it also appears that some people are just much more attracted to violating the rules of society whether it is abusing drugs or alcohol, committing crimes, or just "raising hell". The legal system treats criminal acts as a ***personal choice*** and holds those who commit these acts responsible for their actions when apprehended.

In summary then, I think the best answer as to why a person chooses to commit a crime is due to one or more of the following reasons:

1. **He has a conscience that is not functioning properly** if at all;
2. **He has a distorted value system----***the beliefs and values that help him decide what is right and what is wrong are messed up;*
3. **He lacks impulse control so he won't delay what he wants** and wants now.

Still, questions remain:

- Why do some people think about committing crimes they know involve wrongdoing and that will harm other people?

- Why do most people who think about committing a crime reject the idea while others follow through and carry out the crime with little thought of the consequences?

There appears to be what I call a "criminal thinking threshold" that exists for a every person. The **criminal thinking threshold is that point in a person's thinking where the desire to commit a crime becomes stronger than the fears he may have about committing the crime.**

Whenever the thought enters a person's head to consider breaking the law and committing a crime, a decision must be made. There is a thinking process involved. The choice is either...

1. **to put the criminal idea into action and commit the crime;**

or,

2. **to reject the criminal impulse and walk away.**

For most people, the criminal thinking threshold is never reached, even when they consider committing a crime.

But for repeat offenders, the criminal thinking threshold seems to be passed very quickly **if it exists at all** so that there is very little thought given by criminal thinkers to the consequences of committing crimes.

A Criminal Thinker is usually super confident he can pull off a criminal act successfully. **That is why the thought of punishment has very little deterrent effect on repeat criminal offenders**.

That is also why, when criminal thinking dominates a person's life, **it is like living under a curse**, because there is no functioning warning system to hold the person back from making bad choices that bring on trouble.

Dr. Stanton Samenow, PhD, in his book, Inside the Criminal Mind (Times Books, Random House, New York, 1984), wrote about his research based on over 20 years of experience in dealing with repeat offenders in a maximum security prison. He came to the conclusion that ***the thinking processes*** of a person who ***repeatedly*** commits crimes is different from the majority of people who do not commit criminal acts.

This difference in thinking is highlighted in the two kinds of thinking: criminal thinking scenario and the thinking of a person who rejects committing the crime and acts responsibly. These two types of thinking can be compared as follows (based on a summary of the types of responses Dr. Samenow records in his book):

Thinking responses of a person **dominated by criminal thinking**	Thinking responses of a person **who rejects the impulse to commit a crime**
"I obey my own rules-----not other people's stupid rules. Basically, something is right for me if it's what I want, feel, or need to do at the time."	"I know what I want to do is wrong and it will hurt people in the community; If I carry it out, my conscience will bother me and I will feel guilt which I wish to avoid. I won't be able to live with myself."

"My only interest is in what I want and what I can get from the opportunity at hand. Besides, my family are always on my case so I ignore them. I have no job to lose, and no reputation to worry about. So, what other people think doesn't concern me."	"I fear the disapproval of onlookers and society, and I fear the shame my family would suffer if I am caught. It just isn't worth the risk. I don't want to drag my family through this or let them down. How could I possibly explain it to them?"
"It is unlikely I will get caught; and even if I am, it is unlikely I will get prison time. I'm smarter than the cops when it comes to crime and a sharp lawyer can get me off."	"There is a good chance I will be apprehended. If so, I would probably lose my job, my status in the community, and my friends. It would be humiliating for my family and fill me with shame. It just isn't worth the risk."
"I am confident I can pull the crime off smoothly and that I will not be caught. Most other people and particularly cops are basically stupid."	"There are so many things that could go wrong. The victim might be armed or offer resistance; I might be caught. The rewards are not worth the risk."
"By pulling off this score, I will have the money and things I need NOW to lead the life I want to live. Besides, everyone does it. Politicians and corporate executives steal and get away with it."	" By ***not*** committing the crime, I am sparing myself and my family a lot of grief and I will be able to live with myself. I know what I want to do is wrong and it will hurt people in the community."

Other Characteristics of Criminal Thinking

If a person spends of a lot of their waking time fantasizing about the crimes they would like to commit-----theft, robbery, fraud, assault, rape, even murder-----then their mind has probably been taken over by criminal thinking.

This may be true of prisoners who like discussing crimes they would like to commit or enjoy bragging about successful crimes they committed in the past.

It also may include prisoners who are constantly looking around at their surroundings---in or out of prison-----for opportunities to commit crimes, particularly thefts, illegal drug offences, and assaults. Some repeat offenders fall into this class.

If nothing intervenes to break this cycle to change their thinking, then they are more likely to re-offend. It can be an ongoing downward spiral which becomes a way of life. It is what is typically meant by the term, "hardened criminal", a person who has a high probability of re-offending and ending back in prison----repeatedly.

But **the cycle of criminal thinking** can be put in the past and replaced by something much better and more hopeful.

Having said all this, I have no idea how an individual prisoner reading this book relates to what has been stated in this chapter. Every person's circumstances are different. For example, many people in prison are not repeat offenders, but may have only committed one criminal act so that ***much that is stated in this chapter would not apply to them***.

However, nearly every prisoner needs some form of forgiveness, healing and restoration (as do most people everywhere) and every prisoner has to put up with other prisoners who are dominated by criminal thinking. It is a fact of prison life.

As we stated earlier, criminal thinking is just an extreme form of the tendency we all have to choose evil-------as a result of the human nature we were born with because of the rebellion against God by the first human pair.

If you can recognize that this ***is the condition into which we were all born,*** you can make changes to your thinking so that bad choices do not dominate your life but are put behind you----for good.

The Lord of the Universe is a Moral Being that wants people to treat one another with kindness and respect, including respect for their property and their person. That is why God's moral laws were given to humans so that individuals and communities will thrive by being safe and prosperous.

By exploring another path, another worldview, it may help you move your thinking so you will make good choices that can give you a clear conscience and a more fulfilling existence. This is what forgiveness, healing, and restoration are all about. These are themes we will discuss in more detail shortly.

Day 22 Chapter 22: Criminal Thinking *Can* Be Put in the Past and Replaced With Something Much Better

Old habits are hard to change and old thinking habits are even harder to change. This is particularly true of criminal thinking. When criminal thinking becomes the default way a person thinks and interacts with the world, it also affects the way a person responds to other people.

Typically, the responses of a criminal thinker include constantly lying to avoid being exposed, blaming others for anything that goes wrong in his life, and anger, frustration, and lashing out whenever things don't work out as he wished. This tells us that for a person to move away from criminal thinking requires several things:

- Resisting every day the old thinking and ways of responding.
- Adopting a new world view and value system completely different from the criminal world view.
- Changing how he responds to others by rejecting the natural desire to lie, blame others, lash out in anger and frustration----when anything goes wrong in his life.

This is not easy to do. But it can be done. It requires two changes:

1. A genuine desire to change and go down another path.
2. A willingness to work at making changes in his thinking and his responses to others when things don't go his way.

Most psychologists say that it takes about 3 months to drop an old bad habit and adopt a new good habit. Some say the first 3 weeks are the hardest, followed by another two months of tough slogging. **The key is to work at it every single day**. For some bad habits like alcoholism or drug addiction, the struggle to drop an current bad habit and adopt a good habit (abstain from all alcohol or drugs) may last a lifetime.

The key factors for success in moving away from criminal thinking are adopting a new way of thinking, and working at replacing the old ways of responding with new ways of responding. This requires constant effort **day in, day out.**

Keep at it. Don't give up, because there are only three choices facing for a person whose life is dominated by criminal thinking:

1. Stay as you are with your current way of thinking and responding
2. Make a change in your value system, world view, and in the way you respond to others when things are not going your way
3. Avoid both alternatives 1 and 2 and commit suicide

Options 1 and 3 are not good choices and solve nothing. They are very bad all round. In contrast, Option 2 offers hope that things will be better, and it can be done.

Another challenge is that we all tend to seek out and associate with other people who think like us and who we feel comfortable with. Therefore, if a person moves towards criminal thinking, he may feel most comfortable with others who think like him and make hanging out with such people his strong preference.

For example, many prisoners seem to feel most comfortable with other convicts or ex-convicts because they can relate to exactly how other convicts think and act. This can be a real barrier to making radical changes in their outlook when released. This in turn just makes the whole slide into criminal behavior and a criminal life-style much more likely.

Such a person can become "hardened" to sin as criminal thinking becomes his automatic and normal way of thinking. He won't even regard it as "bad" ----it's what comes naturally and what he comes to regard as a perfectly normal way of living and responding.

This is not what God wants for any person and it doesn't have to be this way. He made us "in His image" so that we might reflect His goodness. When a person becomes wholly given over to criminal thinking, then there is little or nothing of God's image that is reflected in that person.

The tragedy is that if this is what we want and if we are not interested in changing, or don't even see it as a problem, then ***He will grant us our wish and let us go our own destructive way***. He will let us "reap what we sow".

When we reach that point where there is virtually nothing in us that reflects His image, then and only then, as a result of our choices, will He ***reluctantly*** abandon us to ultimate eternal separation from Him and His ways. This is what is meant by Hell---eternal annihilation and separation from God. Here is what the Bible says about people who choose this path:

Psa 36:1-3 *There is an inspired truth about the wicked person who has rebellion in the depths of his heart: He is not terrified of God. He flatters himself and does not hate or even recognize his guilt. The words from his mouth are nothing but trouble and deception. He has stopped doing what is wise and good. He invents trouble while lying on his bed and chooses to go the wrong direction. He does not reject evil.*

Such people no longer exist as far as God is concerned. He ceases to have a purpose for them so it is as if they never existed. He can't work with them because they have no interest in Him or in making meaningful changes to their thinking.

Psa 36:12 *Look! Those who do evil have fallen! They are thrown down, never to rise again.*

1 Samuel 2:30 "*those who honor Me I will honor, but people who choose to despise Me, I, in turn, will consider contemptible: those who hate Me will not matter to Me*".

This results in a state that the Bible describes as being "*without hope and without God in the world*".

This is not what God wants for each of us. Instead, what He wants is that we will voluntarily include Him in our life and try to follow His rules so we can have a successful life. He badly wants us to put behind us any wrong-doing and start down a better more hopeful path.

He has provided a way to get there that allows us to be forgiven for real Hope for our future. That is why people also have a natural instinct to seek something beyond themselves----what is usually called a spiritual or religious sense.

These two aspects of our human nature---our one tendency towards corrupt thinking and our other tendency to seek after something greater than ourself, our spiritual sense ----***pull us in opposite directions***.

So, ***what we want to do is*** often in conflict with ***what we sense God wants us to do*** as reflected in our conscience.

What is needed is a reason to move in more positive direction by replacing criminal thinking with something much better.

I believe this is much more likely if we base our thinking on a foundation belief in the existence of the God of the Bible---the Eternal Lord of the Universe, His promises, and His moral commandments.

Day 23 - *Chapter* 23: What Measures Has God Given to Us to Reduce Bad Thoughts and Actions?

In a previous chapter, we talked about the Judeo-Christian understanding of human nature as the cause of why we think bad thoughts and make bad choices----***and every person is affected***.

When we do what is contrary to what the Eternal One wants us to do and instead do what ***we*** want, it is called "sin".

"Sin" is the thing that separates us from the Eternal One and ultimately leads to death. The Bible says in poetic language that sin pays a wage and that wage is death.

All human beings have this tendency to sin and we all commit sins. Therefore, we are all in the same boat----- we are all separated from God and we all die. The first human pair exercised their free will to make a choice that resulted in the "Fall" of Adam and Eve.

However, this separation and death is not what the Eternal One ever wanted as the final destiny for His human creatures. What He really wanted, and what He created us for in the first place was something quite different, something much more positive.

His stated ultimate aim is to fill the earth with His glory:

For the earth will be filled with the knowledge of the glory of the Lord as the waters cover the sea. (Habakkuk 2:14) What does this mean?

God's glory can be seen in different ways. One obvious example is in the natural world. King David wrote in one of the Psalms, "*The heavens declare the glory of God.*" Who has not had a sense of awe when looking up at all the stars on a clear dark night, or at an amazing sunset, or sensed the ominous feeling from an approaching thunderstorm on a lake or seashore? But behind all of these things is God's glory---- manifested in beauty, power, or both. It is through natural occurrences like these that God is able ***in part,*** to reveal His glory to all people no matter their race, heritage or location.

But He intended more than this: He wants to have ***a relationship with each human being*** where He can glory in each person and we can respond by glorifying in Him. That is why it says in the first chapter of the Bible that God made us "in His image". ***He did this so that He could interact with us in a relationship.***

So, while the sin of the first human pair severed the close relationship they had with the Eternal Being and set us all on a destructive path of sin and death, God has opened a way for us to restore the relationship with Him that has been lost due to sin.

His purpose in filling the earth with His glory ***involves human beings who voluntarily respond to him and seek a relationship with Him***. He in turn makes promises of great blessings to this group including ultimately "calling them by His name"---- a way of showing the special relationship He has with this group. The Bible states this purpose as follows: "*God first visited the nations, **to take out of them a people for his name**.*" (Acts 15:14, WEB version)

We will spend the next five or so chapters dealing with the opportunity the Eternal Lord of the Universe has opened up to every person regardless of their past deeds or current state.

If this opportunity is taken hold of, it results in the transformation of human beings on several levels that sets us on a new course where:

- our poor choices (sins) are no longer counted against us;
- we are promised a remedy for the problem of death and dying (extinction of our being) that we all face;
- we have the promise of being resurrected with a new physical body that doesn't die or deteriorate, and of being giv a role in managing a radically transformed earth-------paradise restored (as the Lord's prayer says....."thy kingdom come, thy will be done on earth").

This is what the Gospel of the Kingdom is all about and what we will discuss in more detail in later chapters.

However, before we get to that, I want to discuss the ***"temporary"*** measures the Eternal Being has put in place ***here and now*** to keep our natural tendency to do evil in check so that it doesn't lead to the destruction of human society.

1. A Thinking Brain with a Built-in Conscience

The first measure He has provided us with we have already discussed-----a ***Thinking Brain with a Conscience*** to help restrain us from making bad choices that hurt others.

A conscience is hard-wired into the brain of every human being and usually makes us think about the choices we make. When people in the community have a strong conscience with a good sense of moral responsibility based on something like a belief in the Ten Commandments, then there is little fear of being cheated, robbed, raped or murdered.

Our conscience is our early-warning system that tells us to "back off" when we are attracted to committing a wrong deed that may hurt another person.

As mentioned previously, it is not sufficient in itself to keep us from making poor choices. It must be developed from an early age and we need to learn to listen it because we can all easily override and ignore what our conscience is telling us.

2. God Approves of a System of Justice Administered By Government

The second measure that God has set in place to restrain evil and protect society is a system of criminal justice. He has authorized humans to put in place a system of justice to apprehend, restrain and punish criminal wrong-doing in the community. By this we mean a ***fair*** system of criminal justice that enforces the law (much of which is based on God's moral rules like the Ten Commandments) but provides ***fair*** and just punishment that fits the crime rather than the excessive punishment that is often seen today.

Criminal justice should also include programs that promote rehabilitation so that the offender can be integrated back into the community and can become a productive citizen.

In the Bible, the Apostle Paul wrote about this in his letter to the believers in Rome. He writes,

"*It is important that all of us submit to the authorities who have charge over us because God establishes all authority in heaven and on the earth. Therefore, a person who rebels against authority rebels against the order He established, and people like that can expect to face certain judgment.*

You see, if you do the right thing, you have nothing to be worried about from the rulers; but if you do what you know is wrong, the rulers will make sure you pay a price.

Would you not rather live with a clear conscience than always have to be looking over your shoulder? Then keep doing what you know to be good and right, and they will publicly honor you.

Look at it this way: The ruler is a servant of God called to serve and benefit you. But he is also a servant of God executing wrath upon those who practice evil. If you do what is wrong, then you'd better be afraid because he wields the power of the sword and doesn't make empty threats.

So submission is not optional; it's required. But don't just submit for the sake of avoiding punishment; ***submit and abide by the laws because your conscience leads you to do the right thing.***" (Romans 13:2-5 - the Voice version)

The Biblical worldview encourages people to be morally responsible and to keep their natural impulses to do evil in check. When this condition exists, then society doesn't need the heavy hand of law enforcement to the same extent.

This is because when people recognize that the moral laws are God-given, for our good, and that we will answer to God when we break these commandments, then ***they will be more likely to want to choose good actions and avoid bad ones.***

3. A Faith Community to Help Those Facing Challenges

The third temporary measure that God put in place to restrain evil and promote good was the establishment of groups of Christian believers in the community which is called the Church. This community of Christian believers is scattered all over the world and is not a particular organization or denomination.

It is groups of ***people who are trying to serve God and work for the Kingdom of God***. If they are doing the job God has given them, they should be trying to do the following:

- provide a social network, and support and care for fellow believers when needed;
- preach the gospel of Hope and help relieve suffering, particularly to those who are oppressed, imprisoned, addicted, etc.;
- stand for truth and justice in the wider community.

For example, supposing you just got out of prison and had nowhere to go, and your family didn't want to have anything to do with you and you had little money. There are church organizations in most communities that can provide temporary assistance or direct you to an agency or place where you could get food and lodging, and help you find employment until you get back on your feet. That is because Christian believers are called to be like lights in a dark room.

The positive effect of a Christian faith community can exist, to some extent, even in prison. For example, who would you likely be more fearful of----a group of prisoners who were known to be "Christians" and were meeting together to have a Bible study, or a group of prison gang members who were milling about making plans to assault other inmates?

The point is that any community where the majority tries to follow what the Eternal One wants for human beings should be a community with more harmony, happiness, and less fear.

Day 24 - Chapter 24: Our Corrupt Human Nature: Why We All Need Transformation

Many prisoners probably recognize that the crimes they committed were the result of bad choices. What they don't often understand is **WHY** they made these bad choices.

In fact, if a person never had much religious or moral training, they wouldn't necessarily be aware of the problem of "sin-infected" human nature and **wouldn't view it as a problem in the first place**. It is simply what comes naturally in the way they think and act.

They wouldn't recognize the need for a remedy and would likely reject out of hand any solution, particularly one that seemed to "push religion".

On the other hand, if a person recognizes the root of the problem **is with our corrupt human nature**, something we all share, then he will usually be open at least to consider possible remedies that deal with this problem, one that affects every person.

As previously discussed, the Biblical worldview says that the root cause for making bad choices isn't external factors like poverty, racism, etc.

Rather, it is our natural tendency to violate what God wants us to do. That tendency has been hard-wired into the brain of every human being ever since the first human pair, Adam and Eve, chose to rebel against the one command God gave them.

As a result, we are all rebels at heart and rebellion against God and His moral laws is our **default position.**

Therefore, **the main struggle that each human faces is the struggle against his own corrupt nature.** It is a struggle with ourselves and our natural inclinations to self-centeredness, seeking constant stimulation and thrills, never-satisfied appetites for sex, drugs or alcohol, laziness, etc. It is often reflected in a desire to rebel against authority and rules (parents, schools, cops, etc.).

While this is part of the Biblical worldview, it is not primarily bad news because it is not the end of the story. Instead, the Biblical Worldview holds out the promise of very Good News----which is the meaning of the word, gospel.

The Gospel provides a remedy (which we will discuss in more detail in the next few chapters) that can free us from the pain, guilt, and sense of worthlessness resulting from poor choices in our past.

In addition, the Biblical worldview provides us with a framework or reference point so that our conscience causes us to reflect on our plans so that bad thoughts won't repeatedly lead to bad choices.

This "moral framework" allows us to develop our conscience so that it holds us back from carrying out acts of wrongdoing. **God's laws give us a moral compass to guide our choices.**

This moral compass allows us to make real changes in our thinking to lead us to a more successful way of living. The Biblical worldview also provides us with a means of overcoming guilt, anger, a sense of worthlessness, and all the negative thinking that is a fact of life for many prisoners.

In fact, the Biblical worldview of human nature (also called the Judeo-Christian worldview) has been the underlying basis for Western civilization. While it has been considerably weakened in the last 50 years, it is still the basis for our system of criminal justice. That is why the legal system holds people accountable for the crimes they commit.

But the Biblical Worldview also teaches that no person is helpless or a captive to their nature, with no way out.

Instead, each person is regarded by the Eternal Being as having both free will and dignity. Therefore, each person has the ability to take charge of his own situation. With help and encouragement from others, **he can use his human will and make positive changes to his thinking, outlook, and actions**.

That is, every person ***can*** be transformed to something much better.

The Biblical worldview includes a set of foundation beliefs that act as a roadmap to help any person make practical changes to his thinking and behavior. All that is needed is the will to follow through and start down a different path.

We will expand on this in more detail in the chapters that follow.

Day 25 - Chapter 25: Why Did God Decide to Give Human Beings Free Will When it Often Results in Much Evil and Suffering?

We have already said there can be no human "goodness" without the possibility of human "badness". This is why God has allowed humans to act contrary to what He wants for them---***if they choose to do so***. That is the price He had to pay in order to allow human beings to have free will choice.

He had to voluntarily limit His own power so that people might enjoy the genuine freedom to choose their own course without being under any forced requirement to obey Him. They are free to deny He exists, oppose Him, ignore Him, or rebel against His laws and His purpose.

He must have known that more good would come about by allowing people to have this freedom of choice. Why? Because it appears that **by allowing people to make evil choices, He also allowed people to make good choices** by choosing things like kindness, honesty, compassion, giving of our time or money to help others, etc.

For example, certain good "virtues" could not exist without evil being present because they develop from the need to make moral choices. These include things like heroism, compassion, forgiveness, courage, patience, perseverance, faithfulness, loyalty, and obedience.

Even being in prison may have a good side in that it causes a prisoner to stop and reflect on where his life is going. Some prisoners have told me they would never have changed course if they had not experienced prison.

In spite of some potential good, it is hard to argue that a greater good can result from any single act of evil, such as the abduction, rape, and murder of a child. In fact, we might be tempted to ask, "Has God's allowing evil really been worth it?"

We might be willing to admit that good can come out of evil actions but does the measure of good more than balance out the amount of evil in the world? Only God is in a position to answer that question because He alone has the perspective to see the whole situation in all times and in all places.

He obviously thinks that overall, the "good" is going to outweigh the "evil" in the eternal scheme of things.

It is probably true for most people that when things are going well for us, we don't have much need for God and we tend to ignore both Him and His thinking. But when things go bad for us or our life is threatened or we are in pain due to some illness, or suffer a calamity such as a natural disaster, or someone seeks to harm or kill us----then our need for Him is much greater because we may feel helpless, or our situation seems hopeless.

He wants any interest we show in Him to be a **voluntary** response and **without being forced or coerced**. That is why He remains distant and somewhat hidden from the world He created.

It would appear that if His existence was obvious and "in our face" all the time, then our response to Him would almost be automatic. It would not be a real choice requiring faith and trust—-two things God wants from us.

God wants every person to make a choice either to seek after Him and try to follow His moral commands, or to go their own rebellious way and deny His Existence, ignore Him, and treat His moral commands as if they don't exist.

In other words, every person can do what he wants, when he wants, and how he wants---without any reference to God or His laws.

Or, he can make a conscious choice by including Him in his life. In practical terms, this means having regular contact with Him by talking to Him in prayer and seeking to follow His basic moral commands as a sign of respect.

The choice is for you, me and every person to make.

Day 26-Chapter 26: What Are the Basic Things Most People Want in Their Lives?

In a previous chapter, we discussed why people tend to mess up particularly after thinking bad thoughts which often lead to bad actions.

Most people realize that they fall short of the person they would like to be. This is a problem for everyone. Why? Because our own selfish desires----**what we want**----take over. This shows up in our actions as anger, jealousy, impatience, laziness, envy, hate, lust or greed.

Two problems facing every person could be stated as follows:

Problem #1: Dealing With Our Personal Tendency to Choose "Sinful" Actions

Bad things happen because we are born with a sin-prone nature causing us to often choose bad actions rather than good. Criminal thinking is just a more extreme form of choosing bad actions which involves breaking the law of the land. It is the exact opposite of the God-given "golden rule" that says, "*Do unto others as you would have them do unto you.*"

Even when there is no criminal act involved, we all do things we are not proud of and that we usually regret after the fact. In light of this, **every person needs hope that these flaws and bad actions can be overcome or forgiven.** We can't change the past but we always hope that the regret and guilt we feel for some of our past actions that caused hurt for others can somehow be remedied. Only then can we truly find positive purpose and meaning in our life.

In short, **we all hope that we can become something better than we currently are**----if only to have a better feeling about our own self-worth and to gain the respect of the people we associate with.

For prisoners, this personal longing would likely include the desire to obtain freedom and lead a "normal" life --- one free from control by the criminal justice system, a life free from guilt and shame, from addictions, from having to constantly look over one's shoulder, and to be free of being labelled "convicted felon" or ex-con.

Most people want to have relationships that allow them to love and be loved, perhaps have a family, and a comfortable life with a job where they can earn a steady living wage with proper housing, access to good healthcare, and travel to interesting places.

But for many in prison, these things may seem like a distant dream that is far out of reach. As a result, a sense of hopelessness and frustration may set in along with all kinds of negative thinking.

This brings us to the second problem that all human beings face:

Problem #2: Sin As It Shows up on a Group Basis in the Wider Society

This includes things like inequality, unfair treatment, blocked opportunities, poverty, racism, and corruption.

If you were to ask most people on this Earth what their most basic needs were, you would get a variety of answers---answers that depend on the circumstances under which they are living.

For example, in secure "first-world" countries like the USA or Canada, people might respond by saying their greatest need is to be happy, to have relationships that allow them to love and be loved, and to have a comfortable life with a job that provides a good living wage, proper housing, access to good education and affordable healthcare for their household.

In other parts of the world where hunger, insecurity, or violence are serious problems, they would probably respond quite differently. They would probably say their greatest needs were *to live in safety and security*, *to have a reliable source of nutritious food, and to have access to housing and proper healthcare when* needed for themselves and their families.

Most of the positive things people want are ultimately made possible by good government and a civil society where the rule of law is enforced and respected, where there is equal opportunity for all, and the system of justice is fair for all.

In Canada, where I live, the country came together in 1867. The purpose for forming the country was to provide "*peace, order and good government*". Such "good government" in turn makes possible protection and respect for basic human rights, protection of private property, a fair system of justice, and the opportunity for a good life for all.

However, of the 195 nations in the world today, probably less than 40, or about 1 in 5, could be said to provide "peace, order and good government". Most of these 1 in 5 would be concentrated in Europe, Japan, Singapore, or in Anglo countries like the USA, UK, Canada, Australia and New Zealand.

For much of the rest of the world, this is not the reality. Instead, corruption, tyranny, disregard for the rule of law, and the concentration of power in the hands of a small elite is much more the order of the day. **These are examples of the corrupt human nature showing up in leaders who strive for the power to exploit and control others.**

When a small group runs the show, the result is societies that are dysfunctional or downright dangerous places to live as well as having widespread corruption, crime and lawlessness, poverty, poor housing, and a lack of employment opportunities that provide a good living wage. That these conditions are widespread is evidenced by the flow of thousands of refugees, particularly from Mexico and Central America to the USA and from Africa and the Middle East into Europe, the USA, or Canada.

These are symptoms of **world-wide problems** which seem just too big or insurmountable for human governments to handle on any kind of **permanent** basis. These problems include dealing with climate change, crime, regional wars, hunger, natural disasters, homelessness, addiction issues, disease, terrorism, exploitation of people, etc., although there are some **temporary** successes.

But the successes never seem to last and the problems return. Conflicts and wars like the war in Ukraine are but one example.

Even in advanced relatively prosperous democratic countries like the United States, there are serious problems for some including access to affordable healthcare, racism, homelessness, drug addiction, discrimination against people with a criminal record so that they can't find work or work that pays a living wage, unfair treatment by the system of criminal justice for poorer people who are given a state-appointed lawyer, loneliness, unhappiness (often expressed as being depressed or experiencing anxiety), family breakups, single parent families with children without fathers, and a low marriage rate----and on and on.

Hence, it is for good reason, the Bible says.....

Psa 146:3 (ESV) *Put not your trust in princes, in a son of man [human beings], in whom there is no salvation.*

And in **Jeremiah 10:23** we read,

(ESV) *I know, O LORD, that the way of man is not in himself, that it is not in man who walks to direct his steps.*

In summary, we have identified two overall problem issues that interfere with people being able to satisfy their most basic needs:

1. **Personal Issues** of dealing with our own sinfulness as expressed in our own weaknesses, fears, and inadequacies which afflict all people to some extent;

2. **Society-wide Issues** confronting every country on this earth----hunger, poverty, disease, regional wars, exploitation, etc.;

These two overall problems are related to one another. How?

Our individual selfishness and corrupt nature that all have to deal with shows up on an expanded scale in whole communities and in society in general. This results in the larger global-scale problems that governments seem unable to solve.

What this means is that **if the problem of sin at the individual level could be fixed, then there is real hope that the world-wide problems can one day be solved**.

This is what the gospel message of the Bible is all about------**providing a solution to these two challenges:**

1. **The challenge of our Sin-prone human nature *at the personal level*----**which negatively affects every human being.

2. **The challenge of corrupt human nature as it shows up *in society as a whole*** when it gets expanded and infects

the whole **community** causing problems like corruption, poverty, crime, addictions and homelessness.

In the next chapter, we will explore how God has responded to these two main problems facing human beings and human societies, and provided a remedy for each, which He has communicated to us through the Bible in the **Gospel** or **Good News.**

Day 27 Chapter 27 What *is* the Gospel and How Can Make My Life Better *Right Now*?

When Jesus came the first time, he came preaching the gospel, which simply means, good news. Crowds came out to hear him. Why did this 'good news' interest them. What was it about?

It appears that it consisted of two main things. These are described in the book of Acts, the book that details the spread of the gospel message by the apostles throughout the Roman Empire.

In Acts 8:12, we read that the gospel that Philip the evangelist preached to the people of Samaria was....

"***the things concerning the kingdom of God*** and ***the name of Jesus Christ***." (KJV)

Likewise, in the last chapter of Acts, we read twice in this chapter what the apostle Paul preached in Rome up to the time of his death. In v. 30, we read, (KJV)

" *And Paul dwelt two whole years in his own hired house, and received all that came in unto him,* ***Preaching the kingdom of God, and teaching those things which concern the Lord Jesus Christ****, with all confidence, no man forbidding him.*"

Therefore, the gospel message appears to have **two parts**:

1. Things about the Kingdom of God;
2. Things about Jesus Christ in his role as Savior.

The "**things concerning the Name of Jesus Christ**" focus on things that relate to every human being **right now in the present**. These include our need to be forgiven for our screw-ups---past sins that burden us down with guilt and that make us feel badly about ourselves and our worth as a human being. This is important because even if those we harmed cannot forgive us, God is willing to forgive us because of the fact that Jesus took on the sins of the world when he died on the cross.

This allows a person to start with a clean slate, where his past sins are no longer remembered by God, where the burden of guilt and shame can be lifted and removed. This in turn allows a person to start feeling good about himself so that he sees himself as a person of value. This can greatly improve his mental outlook and sense of well-being.

This is why this part of the gospel is so important. It can improve a person's life NOW and give them a more positive outlook on their future.

The other part of the gospel message, **the things concerning the Kingdom of God,** is focused on the future**-----the future destiny of every person after they die**---to provide hope and reassurance ***that this life is not all there is to a person's existence.***

However, let us first discuss the part of the Gospel that deals with the "things concerning the name of Jesus Christ" because it is that part of the Gospel that can help make you feel better about your life right now. Then we will talk about that part of the gospel that deals with the Kingdom of God. This is the part which gives hope for our future when we die.

These two aspects of the Gospel can give us a much more positive outlook on life, both now and in the future. That is why the Bible calls it "*God's power to save all who believe*" (Romans 1:16 GNB) This 'power' lies in its ability to change a person's life for the better.

Part 4: The Part of the Gospel that Relates to the Transformation of People----"*The Things Concerning the Name of Jesus Christ*"

Day 28 - Chapter 28: Do We Really Need to be "*Saved*"? Saved from What? It all depends on your view of *Human Nature*

Where did human beings get the idea that we need to "be saved"? Saved from what?

The Bible has a lot to say about **salvation**. It is probably the main topic and is found throughout its pages. Why is this?

The Greek word translated in the Bible as "**salvation**" is about ***deliverance from sin*** and its inevitable consequence**------ *death*.**

The Bible tells us that this is a direct result of the curse that falls on all human beings as a consequence of the actions of the first humans, Adam and Eve, when they chose to eat the fruit of the one tree that was off limits to them.

Adam chose to go his own way and to rebel against the ***one commandment*** that God insisted he keep. When he chose to go his own way and ignore God's way by making his own rules of right and wrong, **he was condemned along with all his descendants to an existence that ends in a life of struggle, suffering, and finally death.**

In other words, **this condemned state of suffering and death was passed on to all human beings**. Romans 5 makes this very clear.

Rom 5:12 KJv *Wherefore, as* ***by one man*** [Adam] *sin entered into the world, and death by sin;* ***and so death passed upon all men, for that all have sinned****:*

And again, in Romans 5: 18-19 KJv "*Therefore as by the offence of one* [Adam] *judgment came upon all men to condemnation; .....For as by one man's disobedience many were made sinners.*"

This tells us that in our natural state, **we have no automatic access to salvation from death---the permanent destruction of who we are**.

Why? Because we are born into a condemned state that Paul described to the Ephesian believers as being ***"without Christ... having no hope, and without God in the world".*** (Eph . 2:12 KJv)

It also is **the root cause for the evil in the world** including crime----fraud, rape, robbery, murder, etc.--- and for illness and disease, famine, pestilence, and for death and destruction due to natural disasters like earthquakes, hurricanes, tsunamis, wild fires and droughts.

Also, as we have discussed previously, this curse also causes every person to have **a natural urge to choose evil rather than good.** That is why people screw up and do bad things that harm both themselves and others.

This corrupt sin-prone nature is with us from the moment we are born and is called "sinful flesh" in the Bible. This separates us from God right from birth but this separation becomes even worse when we are old enough to commit sins of our own.

While God made us with a built-in conscience to help us make good choices, our conscience will only kick in if we know about His basic moral laws----like the Ten Commandments and try to keep them.

The penalty for every person for ignoring these commandments is trouble in our life and finally death----total destruction of our being----unless we do something about it.

If you ask most people if they regard themselves as basically a "good person", most will say "*yes, I am basically a good person*". Even inmates in prison who have committed serious crimes like murder, robbery or rape will say "*I am basically a good person. I have just made some mistakes.*"

That is not how the Lord of the Universe looks at things.

To Him, if you break ***any*** of the Ten Commandments such as you shall not steal, you shall not give false testimony or lie, you shall not commit adultery (which includes both actually having sex with another man's wife and/or fantasizing about having sex with another man's wife), you shall not murder, etc., **then the Bible says you have sinned.**

God regards breaking any of His moral laws as "sin" and that makes a person worthy of death. When you review each of these commandments with many people, they will confess that they have broken one or more of these commandments, with the exception of "you shall not murder".

Since we all sin, then we all die.

The Bible says that **sin pays us a wage**, and **that wage is death**. Without some intervention to change things, we are doomed. In our natural sin-prone state, we tend to **choose evil actions** and **have no automatic remedy for this----what we call salvation.**

This is not our fault but it is our fact. Therefore, it is inevitable that **we all face permanent destruction of our being** after a life that involves suffering and struggle.

Still, evil choices are not a foregone conclusion, but **evil choices are the natural response that human beings make much of the time.** If we choose to leave things as they are in this hopeless state, God will let us do that as one of our free will choices.

The Bible tells us plainly how God regards those who choose to ignore Him, His moral laws like the Ten Commandments, and choose to **live their lives as if He doesn't exist:**

Isa 26:14 (GWv) The *wicked are dead. They are no longer alive. The spirits of the dead won't rise.* You have punished them, destroyed them, and ***wiped out all memory of them***.

Psa 34:14-16 (GWv) *Turn away from evil, and do good. Seek peace, and pursue it!* The LORD confronts those who do evil ***in order to wipe out all memory of them from the earth.***

Since we ***all*** do evil in our natural state, this "bad news" applies to every human---the permanent destruction of who we are so that there is no memory of us by God.

But God didn't leave things there. He offered a way out of this mess, because permanent destruction of our being is not what He wants for people. The Bible tells us that God is not willing that any person should perish in this permanent sense. In 2 Peter 3:9 we read,

The Lord isn't slow to do what he promised, as some people think. Rather, he is patient for your sake. ***He doesn't want to destroy anyone but wants all people to have an opportunity to turn to him and change the way they think and act***. (GWv)

From this, we learn several things:

1. God doesn't want to see the permanent destruction of any person. This implies that all people have value to Him because all human beings were made in His Image. But for this to happen, **He requires that we respond to Him and undertake a change in the way we think and act.**

2. The way out of our hopeless situation is called ***Salvation***. But it is not available to us unless we do something in return.

3. If we seek after God and the salvation that He offers, then He keeps a record of who we are, He remembers

everything about us including our DNA, and this record becomes part of what **He calls The Book of Life.**

Jesus spoke about this in the Book of Revelation.

He said......Rev 3:5 (GWv) *Everyone who wins the victory this way* [over death] *will wear white clothes.* **I will never erase their names from the Book of Life**. *I will acknowledge them in the presence of my Father and his angels.*

In Rev. 20:15, we are told that those whose names are not recorded in God's Book of Life will be permanently destroyed. Revelation is a book of symbols and symbolic language is used:

Rev 20:15 (KJV) *And whosoever was not found written in the book of life was cast into the lake of fire.*

This tells us that those individuals whose names are not in the Book of Life face total destruction of who they are when they die. This is described in symbolic language as being burned up and consumed in the symbolic lake of fire.

Salvation is all about God retaining memory of a person so that He can deliver us from permanent destruction when we die.

So how does this all work out? What if there are many bad things in your past that you can't change? Those things can be dealt with in a positive way. It comes about by means of God's plan of Restorative Justice.

Day 29 - Chapter 29: What is "*Restorative Justice*" and How Does It Work?

I have been a volunteer for the last 11 years in a **Restorative Justice Program** through the John Howard Society involving young offenders between the ages of 14 and 17 who have had a relatively minor scrape with the criminal justice system.

I believe the ***restorative justice program*** has a lot in common with the plan of salvation that God has put in place for his human creatures-----His plan for transforming human beings into something much better.

Let us first describe, by way of contrast, how the "**retributive justice**" or **punishment model** works-----which is **the standard model for criminal justice** in all countries.

1. Characteristics of Retributive Justice---***the Punishment Model***

This model seeks to answer three questions:

1. What laws have been broken?
2. Who is/are the offender/offenders?
3. What punishment does the offender deserve so the victims feel that justice has been served and the community is protected?

The most important aspects of this system are to ensure that only the guilty are convicted and that the punishment fits the seriousness of the crime.

Sadly, in any human system of justice, these two aspects do not always exist for a given criminal case. Sometimes the innocent are found guilty of a crime they did not commit or found guilty of a more serious crime than the circumstances indicate, and sometimes, the penalty does not appear to fit the crime-----it may be too lenient or too harsh.

Also, under this system, the primary aims are for both the victim (or victim's family) and society at large, to feel confident that justice has been done, and that the community will be protected from those who commit lawless acts.

The downside is that there is ***little or no attempt to "heal" the problem that exists between the victim, the offender and the community***. There is little emphasis on restoration of the damage done to the victim or to rehabilitation of the offender so that when he returns to the community, there will be supports in place so that he will not re-off end in the future.

God only uses this punishment-centered approach when a person or a society are unrepentant and unremorseful for serious wrongdoing.

His preferred method of dealing with people is through a system of **Restorative Justice**. This is what the second part of the Gospel is all about.

The Gospel Message as it relates to "the things concerning the Name of Jesus Christ" is about restorative justice-----**transforming human beings into something better**.

So let us begin by discussing how a system of ***restorative justice*** is different from a system of ***retributive (punishment-focused justice)***.

1. Characteristics of Restorative Justice**---*the Healing Model***

The main focus of a system of restorative justice is based on the following premise: Just as *a crime causes harm*, so *the system of justice should promote healing.*

In order to promote healing, ***both the victim and the offender must take an active role in addressing the consequences of the crime.***

Restorative justice solutions actively engage the affected parties:

1. *those who were harmed*
2. *the offender(s)*
3. *the wider community*

All three parties to the crime must be involved in order to **seek solutions that help repair the damage done that promote reconciliation between the parties involved** and to promote the rebuilding of relationships with the community so that such actions do not re-occur.

While a **facilitator** or **mediator** is usually needed to make the process work, the key aspect is that both the victims and the offender ***agree to be part of the process.***

Either the police or the Prosecutor/DA can direct the offender to this program if they admit to the wrong doing and agree to participate in this alternative to a trial, probation or jail time. (If the young person is not willing, the charges would proceed through the courts under the retributive justice model with a possible conviction leading to probation or incarceration.)

The victims of the crime are not directly involved in these cases because of the young age of the offenders. Instead, the volunteer facilitator represents the interests of the victims and the community where the offence took place.

The volunteer sits down with the young person and has about a one-hour discussion about the crime from the young person's perspective (which often differs from the police report which can leave out key details), a discussion about the young person's life before and after the offence, current schooling, part-time jobs, hopes for the future, career goals, what they do in their spare time----sports, hobbies, friends---, and family relationships.

We then jointly discuss and work out three projects for the offender to undertake before their next court date. These projects are called "sanctions" and often include attending a workshop, writing a short essay where they reflect upon what happened and what they have learned from going through this process, or writing a letter of apology to the victim, or doing a set number of volunteer hours of approved community work, or paying "restitution"---(an amount determined by the DA that is equal to the cost of the damage done). The facilitator tries to match the "sanctions" selected to the type of offence, and to the interests and abilities of the offender.

The purpose of assigning the "sanctions" is that by giving the offender tasks to complete that require time and effort, the offender can show that he is committed to the program and wants to learn from his past offences and move forward in a positive way. The tasks selected are designed to promote these outcomes.

The facilitator then has a follow-up meeting with the young person about three weeks later to review the progress in completing the sanctions. When all of the sanctions have been completed satisfactorily----with evidence that the offender has put time, effort and reflection into completing the assigned tasks-----**then the court is informed and the charges are dropped so the young person has no criminal record.**

If more effort and time is needed in completing the tasks in a satisfactory manner, then the young offender will be directed to make changes and resubmit the results for a further review.

This program has about an 85% success rate. That is, 85% of the young people who participate in this program have no further involvement with the criminal justice system for the next five years.

The aim is to break the cycle of ongoing criminal activity by the young person so that they do not go on to commit repeated or more serious offences.

This type of program is made available by the DA for relatively minor offences. It is a very positive alternative to tying up the courts, saddling a young person with a criminal record, and mandating a sentence of either probation or incarceration. Also, it does not tie up the police, probation officers, or juvenile detention personnel.

Restorative Justice programs are not typically used where the person is a repeat offender or where the crimes are felonies.

However, a different form of restorative justice is sometimes used where a person has been convicted of a serious offence and is serving substantial prison time. In these cases, ***if the victim is willing***, restorative justice is sometimes used to bring the victim and offender together in an attempt to achieve some type of closure and reconciliation, for both the offender and the victims. These situations require the voluntary participation of both parties and rely on the expertise of a mediator, and usually take place five or more years after the offence was committed, and when the offender is in prison.

The purpose is to get the offender to recognize the hurt caused to the victims and for the victims to see the offender as a struggling person who very made bad choices. The aim is to promote healing and forgiveness, if possible, so that ***all*** the parties can move forward in their lives by removing some of the mental burdens, particularly anger or guilt, that resulted from the crime.

In summary, Restorative Justice programs have the following common characteristics:

1. **A voluntary commitment to participate** by all the parties affected by the offence----the victim/victim's family, the offender, and the wider community.
2. **An acknowledgement by the offender** that **he accepts responsibility for the offence** he was charged with and **for the harm he caused**.
3. **Completion of certain tasks by the offender** to show both his sincerity in participating in the restorative justice program and his genuine commitment to changing his thinking and behavior away from the thinking and behavior he showed when he committed his crime(s).
4. **A facilitator or mediator** (often volunteers from the community) to assist in helping the parties to heal and be reconciled.
5. **A promise by the state (justice system)** to provide relief to the offender, by dropping the charges upon successful completion of the program so that the young person does not have a criminal record.

Let us now look at how these characteristics of restorative justice fit into God's plan of Restorative Justice for people.

Day 30 - Chapter 30: God's Plan of Restorative Justice For All People---What Being "*Saved*" is About

With the background on restorative justice, the "healing" model of justice, let us now look at **God's plan of restorative justice---**where the focus is not on punishment but on forgiveness, healing, and restoration of what has been lost.

This plan of restorative justice is **helping a person move to a better, more hopeful condition**. This is what salvation or "being saved" is all about.

God wants to bring healing to all people and restore the 'very good' state of the original creation, that was lost when Adam sinned and he and all his descendants were condemned to have a corrupt nature that leads to sin, suffering and death.

Wc rcad in 2Pc 3:9 *The Lord is not slack concerning his promise, as some men count slackness; but is longsuffering to us-ward,* ***not willing that any should perish, but that all should come to repentance.***

This is because **every person is *made in His image* and is therefore valuable to Him**.

In fact, He almost immediately offered a way to restore things to a better state by promising that it would come about through a special human who would defeat sin and death.

In God's plan of restorative justice, there are three parties involved, just like the restorative justice program I volunteer with:

1. **God who is the *victim*** (in that all humans sin ultimately against God);

2. **Humans** who are the ***offenders*** (*sinners*).

3. A **facilitator/mediator** who brings the parties together and makes it possible to reconcile the victim and the offenders. This person is a special human being----*Jesus Christ.*

God's program of restorative justice has things the offender must do to bring about healing.

1. The offender must voluntarily agree to participate in this program of salvation.

2. The offender must agree to certain conditions including his willingness to complete certain tasks ***to indicate his genuine commitment to the program.***

God in turn will remove the sins that belong to the offender so they are no longer remembered. This will restore the offender to a good relationship with Him.

How did God implement this process? God set things in place so that Jesus Christ, His only begotten son, could open a way whereby the two parties----God and human beings---- could be reconciled and a way opened to bring healing and restoration of what had been lost because of Adam's sin and the sins of all Adam's descendants.

Because God made us in the first place, He gets to make the rules on how to bring about a healing process. He decided that since it was the first humans who sinned by rebelling against Him and brought sin, suffering, and death into the world, He would require the sacrificial death of a sinless human to make things right.

He brought this about by giving to the world His only begotten Son, **who accomplished two great tasks:**

1. **Doing God's will perfectly and not sinning throughout his whole life**----to show that ***Sin can be defeated by a human.***

2. Willingly laying down his life as a sacrifice **to take on the penalty for the sins of all other humans.**

God decided if one human being could do His will perfectly and not sin as well as being willing to lay down his life as a perfect sacrifice----**then this perfectly sinless Son could bear the penalty for the sins of all people.**

This opened the way for the sin and death of humans to be removed. That is why the Bible says,

Joh 3:16 *For God so loved the world, that he gave his only begotten Son, that whosoever believeth in him should not perish, but have everlasting life.*

In the Old Testament prophecies we are told more about the role of this "messiah", the suffering servant:

Isa 53:3-4 GNB ***But he endured the suffering that should have been ours****, the pain that we should have borne. All the while we thought that his suffering was punishment sent by God.*

Isa 53:5-6 *But because of our sins he was wounded, beaten because of the evil we did. We are healed by the punishment he suffered, made whole by the blows he received.*

All of us were like sheep that were lost, each of us going his own way. But ***the LORD made the punishment fall on him, the punishment all of us deserved.***

So, God allowed His only son---**a perfectly sinless special human**---to suffer and die **for our sins**.

But, to prove to the world the truth and sureness of this plan of restorative justice, He brought Jesus back from the dead to show that the same thing would happen for all those human beings who choose to participate in this process of restorative justice. They too would be raised from the dead in the future.

The resurrection of Jesus by God after his death on the cross, gives us the confidence that we can trust God to follow through for us as well. By raising Jesus from the dead, God made him the Mediator or go-between, who would bridge the gap between sinful humans and God.

Paul wrote in 1Ti 2:5 GWv "*There is one God. There is also one mediator between God and humans---**a human, Christ Jesus**.*"

In any reconciliation, ***a mediator*** has to fairly represent and understand both sides.

Only Jesus was able to do this because he knew what it was like to be a sin-prone human. But he also had a very close relationship with God his father and a oneness of mind with his Father that was far greater and closer than that of any other person. We do not have this same ability. **That is why Jesus was a very special human being.**

In addition, he was unjustly condemned and executed by a corrupt system of justice under the Romans. As a result, He knows first hand what it is like to be humiliated, despised by others, and suffer humiliation by the system of justice.

In the book of Hebrews, the writer states, Heb 4:15 GWv "***We have a chief priest who is able to sympathize with our weaknesses**. He was tempted in every way that we are, but he didn't sin.*"

In addition, the Bible says that Jesus "*didn't need anyone to tell him what people are like. He already knew why people do what they do.*" (John 2:25 NIRV). He has great insight into human beings----their fears, their struggles, their failures, etc.

This is why **He will be a compassionate judge and king**.

However, like the Restorative Justice program that I volunteer with, a young offender must agree to voluntarily participate in the program and perform certain tasks to show that he is genuinely committed to the program.

Only then will the Court waive the charges against him so that he has no criminal record. Otherwise, the punishment model of justice takes over and the young offender's criminal record remains on the books.

God's plan of Restorative Justice is no different.

He wants people to voluntarily commit to His program and to show Him that their commitment to it is genuine by making changes to their thinking and actions. If they do this, they will receive all the life-giving benefits of His plan of Restorative Justice.

Day 31 - Chapter 31: The Healing Power of God's Forgiveness

Today fewer and fewer people believe in the God of the Bible. As a result, they don't acknowledge Him as being important in their life or the moral code which claims to be from Him. They also deny that they answer to Him for the choices they make in their life.

Instead, many people today think **they can decide for themselves what is right or wrong based on what they feel and answer only to themselves for what they do** (except of course, if they break the laws of the land and are arrested by the criminal justice system). This is the same attitude that Adam and Eve showed when they rebelled against God.

Deciding for yourself based on feelings is completely unlike a fixed set of moral rules from a Higher Being that apply to all people in all places for all time. Feelings change.

But absolute moral principles like the Ten Commandments do not change. They hold true for all times and all places.

Setting your own moral rules doesn't do away with the problem of guilt feelings because we all still have a conscience.

Also, when people no longer believe in a loving God--- the Eternal One, the Lord of the Universe who gave us the moral laws and who is willing to extend His mercy, grace and forgiveness to us, **then there is no Higher Being for them to go to for forgiveness** and the removal of guilt feelings.

What is more, as we discussed in the previous chapter, true forgiveness can only come about if there is an acknowledgement of wrongdoing that needs to be forgiven.

Forgiveness means our past deeds are completely removed and blotted out so that no record of them exists in God's mind.

And God is anxious to forgive us if we are willing to change course and include Him in our lives.

Jesus drove home this message in one of his parables, the Parable of the Lost Son which we briefly mentioned in one of the early chapters of this book. Here is the account again in Luke's gospel: Luk 15:10-22 (GWv)

Parable of the Lost Son

"I can guarantee that God's angels are happy about one person who turns to God and changes the way he thinks and acts."

Then Jesus said, "A man had two sons. The younger son said to his father, 'Father, give me my share of the property.' So the father divided his property between his two sons.

After a few days, the younger son gathered his possessions and left for a country far away from home. There he wasted everything he had on a wild lifestyle.

He had nothing left when a severe famine spread throughout that country. He had nothing to live on. So he got a job from someone in that country and was sent to feed pigs in the fields. No one in the country would give him any food, and he was so hungry that he would have eaten what the pigs were eating.

"Finally, he came to his senses. He said, 'How many of my father's hired men have more food than they can eat, while I'm starving to death here? I'll go at once to my father, and I'll say to him, "Father, I've sinned against heaven and you. I don't deserve to be called your son anymore. Make me one of your hired men."

"So he went at once to his father. While he was still at a distance, his father saw him and felt sorry for him. He ran to his son, put his arms around him, and kissed him. Then his son said to him, 'Father, I've sinned against heaven and you. I don't deserve to be called your son anymore.'

"The father said to his servants, 'Hurry! Bring out the best robe, and put it on him. Put a ring on his finger and sandals on his feet. Bring the fattened calf, kill it, and let's celebrate with a feast. My son was dead and has come back to life. He was lost but has been found.' Then they began to celebrate."

What does this parable tell us?

In the parable, *the father who* is so anxious to receive his wayward son back, who runs out to greet him, who is anxious to forgive him, and even honor him with a banquet-----**this father represents God**.

This parable tells us that God **strongly desires every person to turn their life in another direction,** to admit wrongdoing where applicable, and include God in their life----so they can receive forgiveness and a fresh start.

The only persons that can truly forgive an offender are the victims of the crime. Unfortunately, many victims refuse to ever forgive the offender, and, in the case of murder or manslaughter, the victim is not around to offer forgiveness. This means that forgiveness of the offender is not available or possible so that the offender must continue to cope with feelings of guilt and regret.

With God, things are different. It is true that God is a "victim" when we break one of His laws because we are committing an offense first and foremost against Him----what we call **sin.**

But, unlike human victims of a crime, **He is willing and anxious to forgive us IF we....**

- Make a sincere confession by taking responsibility for our wrongdoing and expressing true regret for our actions.
- Make a genuine commitment to change our thinking and actions and move our life in a different direction.

This holds true even if the victim can't or isn't around to forgive us. This is what true repentance is all about.

And once we have confidence that God has forgiven us, ***we can in turn forgive ourselves***. This provides us with a great sense of relief because it lifts an immense psychological burden---the burden of feeling guilt---- so we can then move forward in a much more positive way, even in prison.

Let us look a real example from the Bible to see how even major criminal acts like murder can be forgiven.

Case of King David – *'a man after God's own heart'*

David was the shepherd boy who slew the giant Goliath and later became the second King of the nation of Israel, in about 700 B.C. He was a warrior king who fought many enemies but was faithful in his service to the Eternal One except for one serious misstep .

One evening, he looked out from a porch of his palace near dusk which was at the high point in the city of Jerusalem. He saw a beautiful woman named Bathsheba bathing on the porch of a much more humble home below his palace.

He made inquiries about her and demanded that she be brought to the palace. There he had sexual relations with her---something he could command since he was the king.

As it turned out, she was the wife of one of his officers, who was away at the front fighting one of King David's military campaigns against enemies. When a month or so later, she sent word to David that she was pregnant, he immediately recalled her husband, Uriah, from the war front, and told him to take a few days leave to be with his wife.

However, Uriah refused to do this when his men were still in danger at the front. As a result, Uriah returned to the front without sleeping with his wife.

King David was now in a real dilemma, so he conceived an evil plan and ordered his top commander at the front to place Uriah in the forefront of the battle, and then intentionally withdraw from him so that he would be killed. This is exactly what happened, and Uriah was killed in battle. Hence, King David was not only guilty of **adultery**, but also of **pre-meditated murder**.

The Bible is very clear on the penalty for pre-meditated murder: the state is permitted to take the life of a person convicted of pre-meditated murder:

Gen 9: 5-6 " *I will demand the life of any person who kills another person. Whoever sheds human blood, by humans his blood will be shed, because in the image of God, God made humans.*" Also, the Bible states seven actions that God hates (sometimes called the seven deadly sins). One of them is "*hands that shed innocent blood*" (Prov. 6:17).

King David was certainly guilty of pre-meditated murder and of shedding innocent blood, even if it was not done by his own hand. As king, he commanded it to happen.

So how did God deal with him? King David had been a devoted follower and believer in the Eternal One up to this point and was even called by God "*a man after God's own heart.*" Based on this God sent the prophet Nathan to confront King David concerning his very serious sins.

Nathan confronted the king by telling a story. This is recorded in 2 Samuel 12: 1-14:

So the LORD sent Nathan to David. Nathan came to him and said, "There were two men in a certain city. One was rich, and the other was poor. The rich man had a very large number of sheep and cows, but the poor man had only one little female lamb that he had bought. He raised her, and she grew up in his home with his children. She would eat his food and drink from his cup. She rested in his arms and was like a daughter.

"Now, a visitor came to the rich man. The rich man thought it would be a pity to take one of his own sheep or cattle to prepare a meal for the traveler. So he took the poor man's lamb and prepared her for the traveler."

David burned with anger against the man. "I solemnly swear, as the LORD lives," he said to Nathan, "the man who did this certainly deserves to die! And he must pay back four times the price of the lamb because he did this and had no pity."

"***You are the man!***" *Nathan told David. "This is what the LORD God of Israel says: I anointed you king over Israel and rescued you from Saul. I gave you your master Saul's house and his wives. I gave you the house of Israel and Judah. And if this weren't enough, I would have given you even more. Why did you despise my word by doing what I considered evil? You had Uriah the Hittite killed in battle.*

You took his wife as your wife. You used the Ammonites to kill him. So warfare will never leave your house because you despised me and took the wife of Uriah the Hittite to be your wife.

"This is what the LORD says: I will stir up trouble against you within your own household, and before your own eyes I will take your wives and give them to someone close to you. He will go to bed with your wives in broad daylight. You did this secretly, but I will make this happen in broad daylight in front of all Israel. "

Then David said to Nathan, "I have sinned against the LORD."

Nathan replied, "The LORD has taken away your sin; you will not die. But since you have shown total contempt for the LORD by this affair, the son that is born to you must die.[11]

Because David made a full confession of his sins--sins against God as well as against the family of Uriah, and made no excuses, **God forgave him and did not demand that the death penalty be carried out.**

However, although God forgave David, **His justice demanded that He still punish David for his serious wrongdoing**. The child he fathered by Bathsheba died. In addition, after that David faced constant warfare both by external enemies and by conspiracies within his own family---which continued until his dying day.

That is how God works. He is anxious and willing to forgive us of even serious crimes .....

1. ***If*** a guilty person makes full confession ***with no excuses*****-----** that he sinned against the Eternal One, broke his laws, and caused serious harm and suffering to other people.

2. ***If*** a guilty person accepts his punishment as right and just.

3. **If** a guilty person makes a genuine ongoing commitment to change his thinking and actions in order to make a complete break from the past life of committing crimes.

In other words, he must be willing to make a full confession of wrongdoing and a genuine commitment to change his thinking and actions----which is called **repentance.**

If he is willing to do this, then God will forgive him. But if he doesn't sincerely follow through, then forgiveness can be withdrawn.

King David followed through with all of these things. That is why he was forgiven and could write these words in one of the Psalms he wrote:

Psa 103:8-9 The LORD is compassionate, merciful, patient, and always ready to forgive. He will not always accuse us of wrong or be angry with us forever.

Psa 103:10 He has not treated us as we deserve for our sins or paid us back for our wrongs.

Psa 103:11-12 As high as the heavens are above the earth that is how vast his mercy is toward those who fear him. As far as the east is from the west- that is how far he has removed our rebellious acts from himself.

Psa 103:13-14 As a father has compassion for his children, so the LORD has compassion for those who fear him. He certainly knows what we are made of. He bears in mind that we are dust.

The prophet Nathan told David that because he had repented, God would forgive him.

King David felt a great burden had been lifted from his life and he expressed this in two Psalms he wrote about being forgiven for pre-meditated murder (1st degree murder in modern terms), and adultery. The first one expresses his repentance in the form of a prayer to God. Here is what he wrote.....(Psalm 51 GWv)

Psalm 51: 1-2 *Have pity on me, O God, in keeping with your mercy. In keeping with your unlimited compassion, wipe out my rebellious acts. Wash me thoroughly from my guilt, and cleanse me from my sin.*

Psa 51:3-4 *I admit that I am rebellious. My sin is always in front of me. I have sinned against you, especially you. I have done what you consider evil. So you hand down justice when you speak, and you are blameless when you judge.*

Psa 51:5-6 *Indeed, I was born guilty. I was a sinner when my mother conceived me. Yet, you desire truth and sincerity. Deep down inside me you teach me wisdom.*

Psa 51:9-10 *Hide your face from my sins, and wipe out all that I have done wrong. Create a clean heart in me, O God, and renew a faithful spirit within me.*

Psa 51:11-13 *Do not force me away from your presence, and do not take your Holy Spirit from me. Restore the joy of your salvation to me, and provide me with a spirit of willing obedience. Then I will teach your ways to those who are rebellious, and sinners will return to you.*

Psa 51:14 *Rescue me from the guilt of murder, O God, my savior. Let my tongue sing joyfully about your righteousness!*

Any person can be forgiven and have a better feeling about himself and his life---- a life where the burden of guilt feelings is lifted.

Forgiveness means that God no longer remembers our sins. They are gone forever. That is what true forgiveness is all about. That is why David also penned a second Psalm after the prophet Nathan told him that God had forgiven him for the pre-meditated murder of Uriah and the adultery against Uriah's wife. Here is what he wrote:

Psa 32:1-2 GWv *Blessed is the person whose disobedience is forgiven and whose sin is pardoned. Blessed is the person whom the LORD no longer accuses of sin and who has no deceitful thoughts.*

Psa 32:3-5 *When I kept silent about my sins, my bones began to weaken because of my groaning all day long. Day and night your hand lay heavily on me. My strength shriveled in the summer heat.*

I made my sins known to you, and I did not cover up my guilt. I decided to confess them to you, O LORD. Then you forgave all my sins

Then David issues an appeal to others who have committed serious sins:

Psa 32:9-10 *Don't be stubborn like a horse or mule. They need a bit and bridle in their mouth to restrain them, or they will not come near you." Many heartaches await wicked people, but mercy surrounds those who trust the LORD.*

When any person chooses to repent for past wrongdoing, transforms his thinking to a Biblical worldview, accepts that God is the Source of all morality and chooses to take his life in a new direction, then the door is wide open to receive the Power of God's Forgiveness.

Day 32 - Chapter 32: Consider Including a Biblical Worldview As Part of Your Thinking

In the Restorative Justice program we discussed a few chapters back, we stated that anyone who wishes to participate in such a program must be willing to make some changes---particularly to their thinking and actions.

Most of the needed changes involve a person's **moral thinking----**which shows up as our **attitudes**, and **values,** particularly in the way we think we should treat **other people and their property.**

The foundation for our moral thinking is called our **Worldview**, as we discussed earlier. Our worldview explains how we understand the world and the people in it *really work*.

As we have stated earlier, some prisoners have a negative worldview that looks something like this and that shows up as criminal thinking:

- It's a "dog eat dog world" with no purpose or meaning. It's every man for himself-----survival of the fittest.
- No one is going to give me the things that make for a decent life; in fact, others have denied me the things I want and feel I have right to. There is no Higher Being or no one else to look out for me, so if I don't look out for myself, who will? I make my own rules and follow my own code---not the rules others try to force on me. I will do what it takes to get my fair share of what I want, need and am entitled to.
- If an opportunity presents itself, I will rob, steal, defraud, lie, assault, rape and even murder-------if necessary----to get what I want or need.

Since our Worldview is our foundation thinking about how we look at both the present and future, it influences how we live our life.

If we view our future in a positive way, we will behave in a way that reflects that. If we view our future in negative terms with a distorted worldview, we may be stuck with a “f--k the world” mindset and our actions will reflect that.

When our worldview is distorted, it is much more likely that our moral values and attitudes will be screwed up----particularly in the way we treat other people and their property. Then we will make bad choices that constantly mess up our life.

Instead, I believe things go much better for people in life if they include the Biblical Worldview as the main basis for their moral values.

In addition, a Biblical Worldview can help a person gain a perspective on their current situation so that they see things in more positive terms and don’t regard their present circumstances as hopeless, or as the way of defining who they really are.

So let us review the main features of the Biblical Worldview---things we have been discussing in previous chapters:

1. There is a Supernatural Mind/Power who is the **First Cause**-----the Creator and Sustainer of the Universe and the Creator of all living things on planet Earth. This Being we call God---the Eternal Lord of the Universe. (Gen. 1:1)

2. God, created the Earth as a place uniquely suited for living things and hence must have had a purpose for doing so. (Isaiah 45:18)

3. He made one species of animal----human beings--- "**in His own image**" and gave them control over all other animals. In particular, He made them to walk upright, with a unique ability to communicate with both spoken and written speech using language, and to be the only species with the ability to interact and form a relationship with Him.

4. He communicated with the first human pair, Adam and Eve, and gave them one rule that He wanted them to follow: Do not to eat the fruit of a given tree. However, Adam and Eve chose to rebel and disregard the one law He gave them. Instead, they chose to rely on their own sense of what is right and wrong. As a result, the "very good" state of harmony that existed in the original creation came to an abrupt end and was replaced with **chaos and disorder throughout all of nature.**

5. All of Adam's descendants were also given a corrupt nature with a tendency to choose evil actions. In addition, He gave every person a measure of freewill so that they can choose to obey, to ignore or to rebel against His moral laws.

6. While evil actions are not inevitable, evil actions will be much more likely in a person's life unless he learns about and tries to follow the moral laws God has given us like the Ten Commandments, and recognizes that each individual answers to Him for the choices they make.

7. Despite the rebellion by the first human pair, God told them that He had a plan to eventually undo the chaos and disorder that their choices brought on, and **to eventually restore all things to the good state that existed prior to the bad choice of the first human pair**. He revealed that

this plan would be worked out through a special human being----a Promised One.

The Bible then tells us about the **Promised One** or **Messiah** who would be God's only begotten son, who, through a life of perfect obedience, **would make up for the failures of all other persons**. But, in order to show that God condemns sinful actions, His plan would involve the voluntary death of His only begotten but sinless Son, ------in order for him to bear the punishment for the sins of all people.

8. God's Plan of Restorative Justice will reach its climax when Jesus the Christ, returns to Earth at some future date to raise and judge the dead, give an immortal body to those who have chosen to commit to His plan of restorative justice.

In summary, this Biblical Worldview tells us that human existence has meaning and that human history has a purpose. It is moving towards a glorious future here on Planet Earth for people who choose to respond to God's plan of Restorative Justice.

Day 33 - Chapter 33 : A Biblical Worldview Can Help Us Make Better Choices

Jesus urged his followers to work at transforming their thinking so that it more closely reflects the thinking of what the Lord of the Universe wants for us. The Biblical Worldview gives us a realistic foundation to help guide our thinking.

We all need to abandon our selfish thinking and replace it with something new. Jesus challenges us to move our thinking in a different direction starting with trying to keep the two great commandments:

1. **Love God** with all your heart and mind---How? by seeking Him out and by **trying** to follow His moral laws in your life. The apostle Peter wrote, "*loving God means keeping his commandments, and his commandments are not burdensome*" (1 John 5:3 NLT). **What God wants to see is that we are trying to move in this direction.**

2. **Love your neighbor** (includes all the people you come in contact with) **as you love yourself**. How? By trying to do good things for your neighbor----instead of being a threat, a person who causes harm, a predator, or a thief. Again, the key is that you are trying to make a change.

   And you don't have to like your neighbor to show this kind of love because it is not a feeling. It is about how you choose to act towards other people---by seeking to do good for them.

The same requirement is found in the Old Testament where the things God requires of all people are clearly set down in the book of Micah, chp 6 at v. 8 ESV:

He [God] *has told you, O man, what is good; and what does the* LORD *require of you but to do justice, and to love kindness, and to walk humbly with your God.*

This means that you are **trying** to do the right thing, that you are **trying** to treat other people with respect, and that you accept your need for God because of your own limitations and failures. This approach is good for any person and involves just taking one day at a time.

Each morning you can say to yourself, "*Today I am going to try to do what is just, fair, and right to others---- I will try to be loyal and fair to others, and I won't take myself too seriously so that I get ticked off easily. But I will try to take God seriously by trusting in Him to help on this new path*".

If you can repeat this every day, in a few weeks it may start becoming your normal outlook each day.

Once a person makes this attitude part of his thinking, he may no longer respond in the same old way----with whatever he feels and whatever comes into his head at the time

In fact, Paul uses the verb ***transform*** when writing to the Roman believers, many of whom were new to this way of thinking. He says this concerning those who are open to hearing the gospel message....

Rom 12:1 NLT *Don't copy the behavior and customs of this world, but let God transform you into a new person by changing the way you think. Then you will learn to know God's will for you, which is good and pleasing and perfect.*

This is a life-long process-----something every person has to constantly work at---- we seek to transform our thinking so we can determine what God would want us to do.

Without this, what we typically choose to do is to follow the self-centered desires of our corrupt nature that come naturally to us. Writer C. S. Lewis said, "No *man knows how bad he is till he has tried very hard to be good.*" (from Mere Christianity by C. S. Lewis)

So we have to be willing to recognize that our corrupt nature is *the problem* that causes most of our problems in life, and separates us from God right from birth. This is our fact rather than our fault. In his letter to the followers of Jesus in the city of Rome, the apostle Paul has this to say:

Rom 8:5 GWv *Those who live by the corrupt nature have the corrupt nature's attitude. But those who live by the spiritual nature have the spiritual nature's attitude.*

Rom 8:6 The corrupt nature's attitude leads to death. But the spiritual nature's attitude leads to life and peace.

Rom 8:7-8 *This is so because the corrupt nature has a hostile attitude toward God. It refuses to place itself under the authority of God's standards because it can't. Those who are under the control of the corrupt nature can't please God.*

In his letter to the followers of Jesus in the province of Galatia, he describes the effects that come from this corrupt nature:

Gal 5:19-21 GWv *Now, the effects of the corrupt nature are obvious: illicit sex, perversion, promiscuity, idolatry, drug use, hatred, rivalry, jealousy, angry outbursts, selfish ambition, conflict, factions, envy, drunkenness, wild partying, and similar things. I've told you in the past and I'm telling you again that people who do these kinds of things* [habitually] *will not inherit the kingdom of God.*

By moving our thinking in a different direction, **we replace the things of the corrupt nature** with what are called **the fruits of**

the spirit or a spiritual nature. These are described by Paul as follows:

Gal 5:22-25 GWv *But the spiritual nature produces love, joy, peace, patience, kindness, goodness, faithfulness, gentleness, and self-control. There are no laws against things like that.*

The aim of all this is to make a complete break with following our corrupt nature. The Apostle Paul writes about this in his letter to the believers in Rome:

Instead, when we commit to a change----to follow our ***spiritual nature***----our life becomes modeled on following God's laws and following the teaching and actions that Jesus demonstrated in his life here on Earth at his first coming.

Rom 8:9-10 GWv *But if God's Spirit lives in you, you are under the control of your spiritual nature, not your corrupt nature.*

Paul states in his letter to the Romans that the ultimate goal of every follower of Jesus is to be "*conformed to the image of his Son, in order that he might be the firstborn among many brothers.*" (Rom.8:29)

What God wants to see is that we are trying to make changes in our thinking, and our choices, responses, and actions----changes that show Him that the Gospel Message now means something to us.

This brings us to the final step in the transformation of our thinking that is required: It is called **Repentance.**

What is Repentance?

When a person comes to recognize that God is the Source of all Moral Laws because He alone is a perfectly moral Being, and that He gave these commandments to human beings so they might have peaceful successful lives, then a person is usually much more willing to take responsibility for past wrongdoing and become more open to changing the direction his life has taken. This process is called **repentance.**

When we repent we are willing to do the following:

- **Admit** or **Confess** that we have broken God's moral laws (like the Ten Commandments----you must not murder, you must not steal, you must not commit adultery, etc.) We do this in a private prayer to Him. This opens the path to forgiveness.

- **Acknowledge** any past actions that caused harm to others and their families, and express genuine regret for the harm we may have caused. Again, we do this in private prayer to God.

- **Commit** to following a new path where we will make a genuine attempt to change our thinking away from old patterns and make a real effort to follow God's moral laws and avoid the old way of responding to situations.

- **Ask** God to support us in this new journey and to give us wisdom to make good choices. Only then, can we move down a new path with new thinking and new responses.

These things can be done every day in a personal silent prayer to God. **It is a private matter between you and Him**.

When a person has committed to change his thinking in this positive direction, then God will remember him and the door is wide open for him to receive forgiveness, healing and a restoration to God's favor----what is called **Grace**----even if others won't forgive him or choose to have minimal or no contact with him.

Day 34 - Chapter 34: Transformation of Our Relationship with God and His Son Jesus Christ

The final words Jesus gave to his disciples after he rose from the dead, but before he ascended to heaven, were these words:

Mar 16:15 -16 Then Jesus said to them, "So wherever you go in the world, tell everyone the Good News. **Whoever believes and is baptized will be saved,** but whoever does not believe will be condemned."

This tells us that a person needs to **know and believe what the gospel is all about** in order to obtain salvation. That is why we have spent the last few chapters dealing with the gospel message. In practical terms, this means the following:

- Recognizing **the hopeless state into which all human beings are born** just by being a descendant of Adam and Eve. We are born "in Adam" ------which inevitably results in sin and death----**eternal destruction of our being at our death**---- unless we take hold of the remedy that is provided to us.
- Recognizing that we need **to formally change our relationship with God and His Son Jesus Christ**.

From our birth, our natural state is that we are related **to *Adam*** and our destiny is only death.

In Rom 5:12 GWv, the Apostle Paul talks about this. He says, *"Sin came into the world through one person [Adam), and death came through sin. So death spread to everyone, because everyone sinned."*

But when we become related to Christ, there is a big change. The apostle Paul wrote, (1Co 15:21-23 GWv)

"Since a man brought death, a man also brought life back from death. ***As everyone dies because of Adam, so also everyone will be made alive because of Christ.***

This will happen to each person in his own time. ***Christ is the first, then at his coming****, those who belong to him will be made alive."*

What these references tell us is that if we don't do something to bring about a change in our relationship, our natural destiny is eternal destruction of our being.

In our natural state, we are described by the Apostle Paul as follows:

Eph 2:12 GWv At *that time* [when you weren't a Christian believer] *you were without Christ. You were excluded from citizenship in Israel, and the pledges God made in his promise were foreign to you. You had no hope and were in the world without God.*

But then he adds how we get change this situation:

Eph 2:13 GWv *But now* ***through Christ Jesus*** *you, who were once far away, have been brought near by the blood of Christ.*

We need to become related to the Lord Jesus Christ-----in particular ***to his sacrifice on the cross***----so our sins can be forgiven-----the reason for which his blood was shed.

How do we change our relationship from being related to Adam ("in Adam") to being related to Jesus Christ (being "in Christ")? We do this by……

1. Believing the gospel----the things concerning the Kingdom of God and the Name of Jesus Christ.

2. Recognizing Jesus as our Lord and Savior, pledging to serve him as our Lord, and confessing that God raised him from the dead.

3. Repenting of our past sins---acknowledging our past failure and committing ourselves to change.

4. Being baptized by water baptism into His name of Jesus as a public declaration that we have made a formal break with our past and are beginning a new relationship with God and His Son.

Whenever there is a significant change in human relationships, a ceremony or ritual of some kind is often called for. For example, to be legally married, you must undergo a marriage ceremony performed by a pastor, priest, or government official like a justice of the peace.

Another example of a formal ceremony is what occurred in medieval times, when a young man had earned the right to became a knight in the service of his lord. A religious ceremony was performed as described in the following account:

"The evening before being made a knight, the young man would have a bath to wash away his sins, and put on white clothes and a red cloak. All night he would kneel in prayer before an altar with his weapons laid upon it.

In the morning there would be a Mass in the Chapel with many knights and ladies there. The priest would bless the young man's sword and fasten it round his waist. The young man would take an oath to fight against wrong-doers and to protect widows, orphans and the poor.

Then his spurs would be attached to his heels, and the priest would declare him to be a knight. In rich households there would be feasting and tournaments to mark this occasion lasting for days."

(from *What was the ceremony for making a knight? https://www.abdn.ac.uk/sll/disciplines/english/lion/ceremony.shtml*)

This ceremony would formally recognize the change in relationship between the young man and his earthly lord. He would no longer be just be another peasant with limited rights but a valued member of his lord's household with new rights, privileges, and duties.

A formal ceremony is likewise required for any person who decides to be a follower of his spiritual lord----the Lord Jesus Christ. The ceremony to initiate this new relationship involves being baptized in water.

The ceremony itself is short and simple. The person being baptized sits in a tub of water or cattle trough or wades into a pond, lake or river with the person who is overseeing the ceremony (typically in a bathing suit or boxer shorts). The person officiating asks him if he believes the gospel and has repented of past sins, and pledges to serve his new Lord, the Lord Jesus Christ.

If the person being baptized then says, "Yes" to these questions, then the officiating chaplain says something like, "*Upon this pubic confession and before these witnesses, I baptize you in the name of Jesus Christ for the forgiveness of your sins.*"

This formal ritual marks **a break with the ALL the sins of a person's past**----and **the start of a new beginning**------a clean slate.

By this act, he leaves his status of being related to Adam---called being "in Adam", and takes on a new status of being related to Jesus Christ-----called being "in Christ." His sins are forgiven and he becomes a brother in Christ.

Day 35 - Chapter 35: Choosing to Serve Jesus Christ as Your Lord and Soon Coming King

When a person chooses to serve Jesus Christ, then the final step is to make a public declaration of the change you are making by being baptized "into Christ".

In this transformation, we become a "new man", and discard our old "dead" man. The apostle Paul described how this change takes place:

Col 2:12-14 NLT "*For you were buried with Christ when you were baptized.*

And with him ***you were raised to new life*** *because you trusted the mighty power of God, who raised Christ from the dead. You were dead because of your sins and because your sinful nature was not yet cut away.*

Then ***God made you alive with Christ, for he forgave all our sins.*** *He canceled the record of the charges against us and took it away by nailing it to the cross.*"

And again, the apostle Paul describes this transformation of people before and after they became believers and were baptized.

1Co 6:9-11 NLT "*Don't you realize that those who do wrong will not inherit the Kingdom of God? Don't fool yourselves. Those who indulge in sexual sin, or who worship idols, or commit adultery, or are male prostitutes, or practice homosexuality, or are thieves, or greedy people, or drunkards, or are abusive, or cheat people—none of these will inherit the Kingdom of God.*"

"***Some of you were once like that***. *But you were cleansed;*

you were made holy; ***you were made right with God by calling on the name of the Lord Jesus Christ and by the Spirit of our God."***

As a result of this new relationship of being baptized 'into Christ', a person is eligible to receive all God's promises, in particular.........

1. **God will forgive him of all his sins so He no longer remembers them.**

Act 2:37-38 NLT *When the people heard this, they were deeply upset. They asked Peter and the other apostles, "Brothers, what should we do?"*

Peter answered them, "All of you must turn to God and change the way you think and act, and each of you must be baptized in the name of Jesus Christ so that your sins will be forgiven."

Col 1:21-23 GWv *"Once you were separated from God. The evil things you did showed your hostile attitude. But now Christ has brought you back to God by dying in his physical body. He did this so that you could come into God's presence without sin, fault, or blame."*

When we are baptized, we are no longer "separated from God" but instead are made "right with God". This removes all the guilt we have for past wrongdoing.

2. In addition, when a person is baptized "into Christ", **he is adopted into God's family** and **is counted as being an heir of all God's promises**.

Gal 3:26-29 KJv *For in Christ Jesus you are all sons of God, through faith. For as many of you as were baptized into Christ have put on Christ. There is neither Jew nor Greek, there is neither slave nor free, there is no male and female, for you are all one in Christ Jesus.*

And if you are Christ's, then you are Abraham's offspring, heirs according to promise.

This says that by being baptized "into Christ", we become related to Jesus Christ and are formally adopted into God's family and counted as being His sons and daughters. As a result, we become heirs of God's promises so that we can receive all the good things that God has promised-----promises that were first made to Abraham, thousands of years ago.

1. Thirdly, **if we die before Jesus comes again, God will raise us from the dead when Christ returns**, just as He raised Jesus from the dead after his crucifixion.

Rom 6:3-5 GWv " *Or have you forgotten that when we were joined with Christ Jesus in baptism, we joined him in his death? For we died* [symbolically] *and were buried with Christ by baptism.*

And just as Christ was raised from the dead by the glorious power of the Father, now we also may live new lives. ***Since we have been united with him in his death, we will also be raised to life as he was."***

Baptism into Christ won't make your life instantly better, but it relieves you from the burden of guilt and shame from past actions, and it gives you a new relationship with God and His Son, **so that you can** focus on a much more hopeful future.

This is turn allows you to gain back your sense of self-worth as a valued human being-----valued in the eyes of the Eternal Lord of the Universe as a brother in Christ.

Day 36 - Chapter 36: The Final Change from a *Dying* Body to an *Immortal* Body at the *Resurrection*

The final transformation of human beings is in the future and involves the greatest change of all----**the *resurrection* of faithful believers back to life again** followed by their being given **a new type of immortal physical body** that does not get sick or die.

The model for this new body is **the body that our Lord was given after his resurrection**. Paul speaks of this in his letter to the believers at Philippi in chp 3.

Ph 3:20-21 *We look forward to the Lord Jesus Christ coming from heaven as our Savior. Through his power to bring everything under his authority,* ***he will change our humble bodies and make them like his glorified body***.

In addition, Paul deals with the subject of resurrection and bodily transformation in more detail in the 15th chapter of 1st Corinthians. Concerning this new body, he writes,

1Co 15:43 GWv *When the* [present] *body is planted, it doesn't have any splendor and is weak. When it comes back to life, it has splendor and is strong. It is planted as a physical body. It comes back to life as a spiritual body.*

Those who have embraced the gospel message will be changed **to have a new body that is energized by God's spirit just like the body Christ had after his resurrection**. It is still a physical body but it is sustained on a completely different basis.

This is why the resurrection of our dead body is so important and why it was something that Jesus and the apostles made a central part of the gospel message that they preached. For example, we read that the enemies of the apostles "*...were very disturbed that*

Peter and John were teaching the people that ***through Jesus*** *there is a resurrection of the dead."* (Acts 4:2- NLT)

These transformed humans---called "godly ones" or "saints", will help Jesus, the Great King of Kings, bring under his rule all nations, and then assist him in his rule in the Kingdom of God (which we will discuss starting in the next chapter).

Psa 149:5 -7 GWv *Let godly people triumph in glory. Let them sing for joy on their beds. Let the high praises of God be in their throats and two-edged swords in their hands to take vengeance on the nations, to punish the people of the world,*

Psa 149:8-9 *to put their kings in chains and their leaders in iron shackles, to carry out the judgment that is written against them. This is an honor that belongs to all his godly ones. Hallelujah!*

The political and religious positions of power will be combined so the 'godly ones' become "king-priests".

Rev 1:5-6 *And from Jesus Christ, who is the faithful witness, and the first begotten of the dead, and the prince of the kings of the earth. Unto him that loved us, and washed us from our sins in his own blood,* ***And hath made us kings and priests unto God and his Father****; to him be glory and dominion for ever and ever.* Amen

This will bring into being the 1,000 year Millennial Reign of Christ or the Messianic Age, which is a transition period before death is finally abolished. This is the topic of the next few chapters.

Part 5: The Part of the Gospel Dealing With the Things Concerning the Kingdom of God--- the Future Destiny of the Earth and Your Place in It

Now we come to the second part of the Gospel---the Things Concerning the Kingdom of God. This part is about the future destiny of planet Earth and your place in it. This is about hope relating to the future which will come about at the return of Christ to the Earth.

This will become a reality for a person when Jesus Christ returns to set up the Kingdom of God here on Earth, or when a believer is resurrected from the dead if he has died, whichever comes first.

It is about a person's future destiny.

Day 37 - Chapter 37 : What is the Gospel of the Kingdom of God and Where Will It Be?

As we discussed a few chapters back, the basic dream that most people have is to live in a "golden age" of peace, prosperity and happiness----all over the Earth. This desire has been depicted in varying ways and has been called by various names: the Age of Aquarius, Xanadu, Shangri-la, Utopia, and the Millennial Reign of Christ. (A millennium is 1000 years and the Bible says when Jesus returns to earth, he will set up a world-wide kingdom that will last for 1,000 years)

It is a dream that seems to arise from deep within the human psyche and may have been planted by God as a subconscious need in the very makeup of people------just like the human need to believe in something greater than ourselves.

However, for a believer in the Bible, this dream will find its fulfillment in what Jesus taught----***the gospel or good news of the coming Kingdom of God here on earth***.

Many Christian people think the gospel is simply, "Jesus died for my sins," and "Accept Jesus as your personal savior," so you can go to heaven when you die. However, this is not what Jesus actually spent his time preaching about during his first coming.

Rather, it was his ***preaching about the kingdom of God*** that formed the focus of his ministry. Time and time again we read in the gospel records that he came "*preaching the kingdom of God*".

Many of his parables were given to teach about that future kingdom and that he was its king. That is why just before his crucifixion, he answered the question posed by Pilate, the Roman governor, in the following way: "So *you are a king?" Jesus replied, "You're correct in saying that I'm a king. I have been born and have come into the world for this reason: to testify to the truth.*" (Jn 18:37 - GWv).

A king rules over a kingdom. Shortly before Jesus was born, the Angel Gabriel appeared to the Virgin Mary and promised her that the son born to her would one day be given ***the throne of his ancestor King David*** (of David and Goliath fame).

David's throne was a real literal throne of a real earthly kingdom that existed from roughly 1000 BC to 587 BC**-----**the ancient Kingdom of Israel with Jerusalem as its capital city. This kingdom was destroyed and conquered by the Babylonians in 587 BC.

The prophets in the Old Testament prophesied that it would one day be **restored** *at the coming of the Messiah.* ***To restore is to bring back something that previously existed.***

This is why, after the crucifixion and shortly before he ascended to heaven, Jesus's disciples asked him, "*Lord, is this the time when you're going to* ***restore the kingdom to Israel?*"** Jesus told them, "*You don't need to know about times or periods that the Father has determined by his own authority.*" (as recorded in Acts 1:6-7 - GWv).

Jesus didn't dismiss their question about the restoration of the real Kingdom of Israel----*a kingdom that had existed in the past-*---- as being ridiculous. **He simply answered that it wasn't for them to know the exact times or seasons when this would happen**. He never implied that such a restoration would not take place.

This belief in the restoration of the Kingdom of Israel which in the Old Testament was also called the "Kingdom of the Lord" [God]-----was the common foundation belief during the first three and one half centuries following the resurrection of Jesus.

In Edward Gibbon's famous book about the history of the Roman Empire, The Decline and Fall of the Roman Empire, he states that the accepted belief during this 350 year period was that Jesus would return to earth, the resurrection of the dead would take place, and then he would establish the kingdom of God on earth during a phase which would last 1,000 years-----what is called the 1,000 year or **Millennial reign of Christ**. This is what he says in that book:

"*The ancient and popular doctrine of the Millennium* [the name given to the first 1000 years of Christ's reign in the Kingdom of God on earth] *was intimately connected with the second coming of Christ....It appears to have been the reigning sentiment of the orthodox believers;*

... But when the edifice of the church was almost completed, the temporary support was laid aside. ***The doctrine of Christ's reign upon earth was at first treated as a profound allegory, was considered by degrees as a doubtful and useless opinion, and was at length rejected as the absurd invention of heresy and fanaticism.***" [words bolded by this author] (from Chapter 13, The Progress of the Christian Religion)

What Gibbon is saying is that what was once the basic understanding of the early church about the Kingdom of God became a heresy to be stamped out, once Christianity became the state religion of the Roman Empire.

Likewise, the American historian Will Durant stated the same things in his book, Caesar and Christ, regarding the beliefs of the early Christians:

"*The belief in the Messianic mission, bodily resurrection and earthly return of Christ formed the basic faith of early Christianity.*"' Will Durant, Caesar and Christ: A History of Roman Civilization and of Christianity from Their Beginning to A.D 325, New York: Simon & Schuster, 1972) p. 575

However, this basic belief got changed over time, particularly after 325 A.D, when Christianity was made the state religion of the Roman Empire and Christians had political power.

The new thinking was that the thousand-year millennial reign of Christ did not mean Jesus would physically return to the earth to set up the Kingdom of God. Instead, it meant that ***the spirit of Christ*** would rule the world through the church for a long indefinite period of time until Jesus returned to judge the earth and take his saints to heaven.

In other words, the Biblical prophecies relating to the coming 1000-year kingdom were treated as being non-literal.

This also fit perfectly with the other new doctrine that was introduced-----that the reward of the faithful dead was not to take place at the physical resurrection of the body here on the earth when Christ returned, but instead was to take place when a person died as an immortal soul that went to heaven (for the faithful) or, to Hell, (for the unfaithful).

I believe this significant change in interpretation of the millennial reign of Christ also led to down-playing **the significance of the belief in a physical resurrection of the body at the return of Christ** replacing it with an idea introduced by Plato, the Greek philosopher.

Plato's idea was that every person possessed an immortal soul which, at a person's death, either went to a place of reward for the faithful (heaven) or a place of punishment for the unfaithful (a place which became the Christian "Hell"---a place of eternal torment).

With this change in focus, it appears that the part of the gospel that Jesus emphasized-----namely **the gospel of the coming Kingdom of God on earth** and **the resurrection of the dead-----**got set aside.

In summary, the kingdom of God is about the desires of what most human beings long for: peace, fair treatment by the justice system, order, security, prosperity, social justice, good health, long life, fair laws, honest trustworthy rulers and a government that treats people fairly and with respect.

The Bible teaches that these things will come about here on earth over a thousand-year period in the Kingdom of God under the righteous rule of Jesus the Messiah, the King of Kings----what is called the thousand-year or ***Millennial Reign of Christ***.

This is what the early Christians believed and emphasized.

Let us now explore in the next few chapters what some of these changes or "transformation" that the Bible tells us will take place on the earth during this Millennial Reign of Christ (or, as it is called in the Old Testament, the Messianic Age during the reign of Messiah).

This is based on prophecies given in both the Old and New Testaments.

Day 38 - Chapter 38: Transformation of the Earth---Coming *Political Changes*

In the last chapter we discussed that the Gospel preached by Jesus was all about "the things concerning the Kingdom of God" which deals with the **transformation of the Earth**.

The Kingdom of God will be the political structure that deals with all the current problems facing human societies. Massive changes will occur here on earth when Jesus Christ returns to Earth to set up the Kingdom of God. It will be the be the governing body that will bring about the transformation of existing political, economic, social, judicial and religious systems on the Earth.

This Kingdom is not **in** Heaven but it is **from** Heaven. That is, it is based on ***a heavenly order of things*** rather than a strictly human order of things like we find today but it is ***a kingdom set up here*** **on *Earth.*** That is why we say in the Lord's prayer, "Thy Kingdom come, thy will be done **on *Earth.***"

While we are not given the exact details of the changes that will take place in the Kingdom of God on earth, we are given hints in various Bible prophecies that allow us to make some general comments.

Let us consider some of the aspects of our current society and culture that will undergo transformation in the Kingdom of God.

1. The many political systems of this present earth will be transformed into a single government body that will rule over the whole earth called the **Kingdom of God**.

This Kingdom will eventually cover the whole Earth.

2. It will be will be ruled over by a just and righteous "King of Kings"-----Jesus the great King.

His rule will be beneficial for the masses of people but harsh for wrong doers and for those who will not submit to his just rule.

Here are a few references from the Bible that detail this: David, in one of his Psalms about Jesus, the future Messiah and King, says.......

Psa 72:8 KJv *He [Jesus, the Messiah] shall have dominion also from sea to sea, and from the river unto the ends of the earth.*

In another Psalm, David quotes God as speaking these words to His son Jesus......

Ask me *[the Eternal Lord of the Universe], and I* ***will give you*** [to Jesus, the great King] ***the nations as your inheritance*** *and the* ***ends of the earth as your own possession.*** Psa 2:8-11 (GWv)

The prophet Isaiah was also given a promise by God about the birth of His son Jesus and the role he would ultimately fulfill here on Earth.

A *child will be born for us. A son will be given to us.* ***The government will rest on his shoulders.*** *He will be named: Wonderful Counselor, Mighty God, Everlasting Father, Prince of Peace.* ***His government and peace will have unlimited growth. He will establish David's throne and kingdom.*** *He will uphold it with justice and righteousness now and forever. The LORD of Armies is determined to do this!* Isa 9:6-7 (GWv)

This has not yet been fulfilled and awaits the return of Jesus to Earth.

3. The King will be assisted in his rule by faithful believers.

These co-rulers will be faithful believers from all ages who will be resurrected if they have died (along with faithful believers still living), to help Jesus bring just and fair rule over the Earth. God spoke these promises to the prophet Daniel......

But the holy people of the Most High ***will take possession of the kingdom and keep it forever and ever."*** Dan 7:18 (NLT

And in the book of Revelation, this same group of people from all ages are described as follows:

"....*You bought people with your blood to be God's own . They are from every tribe, language, people, and nation. You made them a kingdom and priests for our God.* ***They will rule as kings on the earth."*** Rev 5:9-10 (GWv)

Faithful believers will assist Christ the King in the administration of the Kingdom of God in roles described as "kings and priests".

4. This universal kingdom and its government will exist forever and not be subject to problems of succession (death of the leader) or of a new political party taking over with all the uncertainty that brings.

The prophet Daniel interpreted a dream that was given to the Babylonian king, Nebuchadnezzar, that was a prophecy about how all the succession of world empires would ultimately be replaced by a universal Kingdom of God's making.

Here is what Daniel told King Nebuchadnezzar.......

"At *the time of those kings [of all the other world empires], the God of heaven will establish a kingdom that will never be destroyed. No other people will be permitted to rule it. It will smash all the other kingdoms and put an end to them. But* ***it will be established forever.***

Daniel was also given another prophecy regarding the rule of the Messiah----Jesus Christ. In the prophecy, Daniel was told concerning the rule of Messiah....: Dan 2:44 GWv

"He was given power, honor, and a kingdom. People from every province, nation, and language were to serve him. ***His power*** *is* ***an eternal power that will not be taken away****. His kingdom will never be destroyed."* Dan 7:14 GWv

This the central message of the good news as it relates to coming political changes in the Kingdom of God. And faithful believers who have been saved by grace will have a part in governing in that kingdom.

Day 39 - Chapter 39: Coming Changes to the System of Justice, the Economic System, and Religion

In the last chapter, we discussed in more detail those aspects of the Gospel that relate to the transformation of the earth and its institutions.

This chapter is a continuation of that and will deal with ***the coming changes to economic, judicial, and religious systems of our current world.***

5. There will be a transformation to **a single set of laws throughout the whole earth that come from a common source and will be applied fairly. This will result in a much fairer system of justice for all people.**

This system of universal justice has always been a dream of most people but has never happened.

In the Kingdom of God, all the laws will come from the capital city, Jerusalem (also called Zion). The prophet Micah was given a prophecy about this coming change.

Mic 4:1-2- KJV "*And many nations shall come, and say, Come, and let us go up to the mountain of the LORD, and to the house of the God of Jacob; and he will teach us of his ways, and we will walk in his paths: for* ***the law shall go forth of Zion, and the word of the LORD from Jerusalem.***"

In addition, political and religious functions will be combined so that the rulers are both kings and priests. They will bring about a system of justice that is uniform, fair and just.

Today, there is much injustice in the world even in Western countries. Poorer citizens do not necessarily receive proper treatment or true justice because often they cannot afford good legal counsel.

For example, public defenders provided by the state often have little interest in the clients they are supposed to be serving. As a result, those who cannot afford their own lawyer are often convicted of more serious crimes and receive much longer prison sentences than they deserve. **This unfair situation will change in the Kingdom of God**.

King David was given a prophecy about how this would change under the rule of Jesus the King of Kings:

Psa 72:12-14 GWv ***"He will rescue the needy person who cries for help and the oppressed person who has no one's help.*** *He will have pity on the poor and needy and will save the lives of the needy. He will rescue them from oppression and violence. Their blood will be precious in his sight.* "

6. There will be a transformation of the Economic Order so that the rich and powerful can't keep people in poverty or deny them opportunities to earn a decent living.

The prophet Isaiah was given a vision of the Kingdom under the rule of Christ the Messiah. He describes what it will be like in that kingdom:

Isa 65:21-23 GWv "*They will build houses and live there. They will plant vineyards and eat fruit from them. They will* not *build homes and have others live there. They will not plant and have others eat from it. My people will live as long as trees, and my chosen ones will enjoy what they've done.* ***They will never again work for nothing. They will never again give birth to children who die young****, because they will be offspring blessed by the LORD. The LORD will bless their descendants as well.*

This tells us that unlike today, people will not lose their homes because of losing their job, they will not work for unfair wages, they will not raise children who die young because of improper access to good food, housing, and healthcare, etc.

7. There will be a transformation **to a single universal pure language** so that all people can communicate with one another and worship the Lord "*with one accord*".

Other languages may continue to exist for a time, but there will be one universal language that all people will understand and use for world-wide communication and for common worship purposes. This will minimize misunderstandings and distrust between different people on the Earth. The prophet Zephaniah was given this prophecy about the future age......

Zep 3:9 (ESV) "*For at that time* [in the kingdom of the Messiah] I will change the speech of the peoples to a pure speech, *that all* of *them may call* upon *the name* of *the LORD and serve him with* one accord."

All these changes will radically transform the current political, economic, religious and justice systems here on Earth under the firm but fair, just and benevolent rule of the great King, Jesus Christ. This is where the history of the world is headed.

Day 40 - Chapter 40: Coming Changes to the Environment of the Earth

In the last chapter we discussed how it is God's intention to change flawed human laws and economic conditions into something much better. The governing body that will make this possible is the **Kingdom of God** under the just rule of Jesus Christ, the King of Kings.

In this chapter, we will discuss changes to *the physical environment here* on *Earth.* The apostle Paul discusses the transformation of the natural physical order of things on Earth by making a comparison between what exists now and what will change in the Kingdom of God.

Rom 8:19-22 (GWv)
Creation was subjected to frustration but not by its own choice... We know that all creation has been groaning with the pains of childbirth up to the present time.

What Paul states here in poetic language is that the creation, that started out being very good, became subjected to 'frustration". We understand this to be referring to the curse that was placed on the earth as a result of Adam's rebellion.

However, Paul states that this is a **temporary condition** that will exist only until the natural world is set free from this existing "slavery to decay". He adds that all creation has been "groaning" up to the present time with the pain brought on by this curse and is awaiting future deliverance.

We know only too well what this "frustration", "bondage to decay" and "pains of childbirth" actually mean today in the natural world:

- droughts, floods, storms, tornados, hurricanes, untimely frosts, and other destructive weather;
- blights and disease that destroy crops or kill livestock;
- weeds that grow faster and stronger than domesticated plants, or insects that devastate crops------all these are things that make it a struggle to get a proper harvest;
- a landscape where large portions of the earth are not suitable for crops and can only support sparse populations like the Sahara desert or Antarctica;
- malnutrition and diseases that kill young children and the elderly like Covid-19, dysentery, Ebola, or pneumonia;
- devastation of large areas of the Earth as a result of man's poor stewardship and mismanagement---for example, deforestation that causes mud slides and erosion of farmland; or destruction of the environment caused by pollution;
- destruction caused by earthquakes, tsunamis (giant tidal waves following an earthquake) or volcanic eruptions as a result of shifting tectonic plates or seismic disturbances.

All these bad things result from the ***"bondage to decay"*** that the apostle Paul says are ultimately the result of Adam's sin.

In contrast, the Bible speaks of a transformation to vastly different conditions in the age that Messiah will usher in. It will be a return to the ***'very good'*** conditions that originally existed in that special part of the Earth called the Garden of Eden, before the Fall of Adam and Eve.

Consider some examples of these changes, most of which are Old Testament prophecies. What the Old Testament calls the **'Messianic Age'** or the reign of Messiah is the same as what the New Testament calls the **Kingdom of God** or the reign of Jesus Christ.

1. **Human suffering caused by infectious diseases, congenital diseases, mental illness, or accidents, will be greatly reduced.**

In Jesus's first coming, his miracles of healing during his ministry gave us a taste of the changes to come. But we have other indications in the Bible that tell us how that many of the medical conditions that we are unable to effectively treat today will be eliminated. In describing the Messianic Age, the prophet Isaiah gives us this description:

Isa 35:5-6 (ESV)"*Then the eyes of the blind shall be opened, and the ears of the deaf unstopped; then shall the lame man leap like a deer, and the tongue of the mute sing for joy. For waters break forth in the wilderness, and streams in the desert.*"

2. **Average lifespan will be greatly increased.**

Isa 65:20 (GWv) "*There will no longer be an infant who* lives *for only a few days or an old man who doesn't live a long life. Whoever lives to be a hundred years old will be thought of as young. Whoever dies before he is a hundred years old will be cursed as a sinner.*"

3. **Infant mortality will be a thing of the past for all parts of the Earth.**

Isa 65:22-23 (GWv) "*My people will live as long as trees, and my chosen ones will enjoy what they've done. They will never again work for nothing. They will never again give birth to children who die young, because they will be offspring blessed by the* LORD. *The* LORD *will bless their descendants as well.*"

All the conditions described here will require a change in the environment so that people are no longer harmed by the chronic illnesses that are the result of disease or accidents that we can't effectively treat today despite the tools of modern medicine.

4. **The Curse that has afflicted humanity since the Fall of Adam will be lifted.**

This will probably happen gradually over time during the 1000-year Kingdom Age, and ultimately resulting in the disappearance of death itself at the close of the 1000 year Kingdom Age.

At this point, it will be true to say there is ***no more curse***. This is made plain in Rev. 22:3

Rev 22:3 (GWv) "*There will no longer be any curse. The* throne of God and the lamb will be in the city. His servants will worship him."

5. **There will be a change in the way that various animals in the natural world interact with one another.**

Isa 65:25 (ESV)"*The wolf and the lamb shall graze together; the lion shall eat straw like the ox, and dust shall be the serpent's food. They shall not hurt or destroy in all my holy mountain," says the* LORD."

Isa 11:6-9 (GWv) "*Wolves will live with lambs. Leopards will lie down with goats. Calves, young lions, and year-old lambs will be together, and little children will lead them. Cows and bears will eat together. Their young will lie down together. Lions will eat straw like oxen. Infants will play near cobras' holes. Toddlers will put their hands into vipers' nests. They will not hurt or destroy anyone anywhere on my holy mountain. The world will be filled with the knowledge of the* LORD *like water covering the sea.*"

It appears that in the Messianic Age in the Kingdom of God, no members of the animal kingdom will no longer be carnivorous so that conditions of violence in the animal kingdom will disappear.

6. **The Earth Will become a Much More Habitable and Productive Place.**

Amo 9:13 (ESV) "*Behold, the days are coming,*" *declares the* LORD, "*when the plowman shall overtake the reaper and the treader of grapes him who sows the seed; the mountains shall drip sweet wine, and all the hills shall flow with it.*"

While this poetic description by the prophet Amos has particular reference to the land of Israel in the Messianic age, it tells us that that **agricultural productivity in that age will be so great, it will take a lot longer to gather in the huge harvest**.

This can only be true if the climate is less extreme and pests and diseases are not the problem they are today. This will reflect another aspect of the lifting of the curse.

Psa 72:16 (KJV) *There shall be an handful of corn in the earth upon the top of the mountains; the fruit thereof shall shake like Lebanon: and they of the city shall flourish like grass of the earth.*

The Psalmist David tells us in this verse that a condition of Messiah's reign will be that grain is grown on the tops of mountains and that the amount will be like the historical fruitfulness of Lebanon's rich valleys.

Today, grain is not typically grown on the tops of mountains so this poetic description indicates that **the physical landscape of the earth will likely be transformed to a much more moderate climate with much more of the earth being habitable and productive for growing things.**

These then are the main changes the Bible indicates will take place in the Kingdom of God to restore the earth to those "very good" conditions found in the Garden of Eden.

Day 41 - Chapter 41: Other *Possible* Coming Changes

This chapter deals with a one last set of possible changes in the Kingdom Age but these **involve more speculation** because the descriptive language used in these prophecies is more poetic or metaphorical and it is therefore more difficult to determine the meaning. They are simply listed here as a matter of interest but not as something that must be believed.

One such prophetic passage which seems to hint at significant physical changes coming on the earth in order to make it more habitable is found in Hab. 3 v. 3-11.

Hab 3:3-11 (ESV) *God came from Teman, and the Holy One from Mount Paran.....He stood and measured the earth; he looked and shook the nations; then the eternal mountains were scattered; the everlasting hills sank low..... You split the earth with rivers. The mountains saw you and writhed; the raging waters swept on; the deep gave forth its voice; it lifted its hands on high. The sun and moon stood still in their- place at the light of your arrows as they sped, at the flash of your glittering spear.*

These verses ***may*** be suggesting the following:

A cosmic disturbance caused by a comet or some other cosmic phenomenon that causes significant changes here on Earth ("rays flashed from his hand and there veiled his power", "the flash of your glittering spear").

This passage describes a shaking of the nations that causes the "*eternal mountains*" to be scattered and the "*everlasting hills*" to sink lower and "*the mountains to writhe*". This seems to imply a general lowering of high mountains.

This appears to suggest a corresponding rise in the sea floor of the deep oceans to form shallow seas ("*the deep gave forth its voice; it lifted it hands on high*").

There may also be a splitting of the continents into many smaller geographical units or islands based on the statement, "*You spilt the earth with rivers.*"

This would allow for the flow of warm ocean currents from the equatorial regions towards the poles without continental barriers that exist today so that the climate in higher latitudes and polar regions would be much more moderate.

Also, the denser cool waters of the high latitudes (Arctic and Antarctic regions) would then sink and flow as cold currents back to cool the tropics resulting in more comfortable tropical conditions.

While these are speculations, they would appear consistent with the more general prophecy made in Isaiah 65.

Isa 65:17 (KJv) "For behold, I create new heavens and a new earth, and the former things shall not be remembered or come into mind.

The changes will be so widespread that the Earth as we know it today will "*not be remembered or come into mind.*" This likely means that ***it will not be remembered with fondness***, because the new re-configured Earth will be a so much better place for human beings to dwell.

These changes may be brought about by the massive earthquakes prophesied in the books of Ezekiel, Haggai and Revelation at the time of the Second Coming of Christ.

And lastly, there is some indication that **the current separation between heaven and earth will be removed and merged into one.**

This might be done at the end of the thousand year reign of Christ. In the closing chapters of Revelation, we read of a time when death, sorrow, and suffering have passed away and **God dwells with human beings.**

Rev 21:3-4 (KJv) *And I heard a loud voice from the throne saying, "Behold, the dwelling place of God is with man. He will dwell with them, and they will be his people, and God himself will be with them as their God. He will wipe away every tear from their eyes, and death shall be no more, neither shall there be mourning, nor crying, nor pain anymore, for the former things have passed away."*

This may imply that the divide that separates heaven from earth merges into one. Today heaven is called "God's dwelling place" and Earth is called "His footstool". These appear to be very separate places but may not refer to two distinct **locations** but rather to two different **dimensions.** That is why Paul could say to the philosophers on Mars Hill,

Act 17: 26-27 GWv "*From one man he has made every nation of humanity to live all over the earth. He has given them the seasons of the year and the boundaries within which to live. He has done this so that they would look for God, somehow reach for him, and find him.* ***In fact, he is never far from any one of us.***"

Likewise Jesus said, (Mat 18:20 GW) "*For where two or three are gathered in my name,* ***there am I among them.***"

I don't think the Lord was speaking in symbols. I think he was expressing the view that He is sometimes physically near and present at such times. **It is just that we cannot physically experience his presence through our normal senses of sight, hearing, or touch**. The same may be the presence of true of angels, who may be involved in our lives as it says in this next reference:

Heb 1:14 (GWv) "*What are all the angels? They are* ***spirits sent to serve those*** *who are going to receive salvation.*"

We cannot see them because **there is an invisible barrier between us,** but they may very well be involved very close to us in circumstances in our lives.

I think a good way to make sense of this is to think of some science fiction stories about time travel to a different era where a person has to pass through some object to get to a different time. The person is able to move to a different time ***dimension-*** ---but not to get to a different location.

We can't cross to that other dimension now, but I believe in the kingdom age, that other heavenly dimension will become one with the Kingdom of God on Earth. Heaven and Earth will become one dimension. While this involves speculation, I think it is something we can think about.

One thing we can say for sure: all these transformations will be so dramatic that every person living on the earth will know the source of these changes and will welcome them.

Part 6: When Will Christ Return and What Signs Will Tell us His Return is Near?

Day 42 Chapter 42: "*When Will These Things Be?*" When Will Christ Return to Earth and Set Up the Kingdom of God?

These questions have been asked by Christian believers for over two thousand years, from the time Jesus ascended to his Father in heaven after his resurrection from the dead.

In fact, his disciples (who were now called 'apostles' after Jesus' resurrection), asked Jesus this very question shortly before he was crucified.

Now while Jesus was sitting on the Mount *of* Olives, *the disciples came to him privately and said,* "Tell *us, when will these things happen?* What *will be the sign of your coming and the end of the age?*" (Matt 24:3)

Jesus *did* give them a number of signs but cautioned them by saying this: Mat 24:36 "*However, no one knows the day or hour when these things will happen, not even the angels in heaven or the* Son *himself.* Only *the* Father *knows.*"

And again, just before he ascended to his Father (after his crucifixion and resurrection, his apostles asked..... Acts 1:6-7 GWv So *when the disciples came together, they asked him,* "Lord, *is this the time when you're going to restore the kingdom to Israel?" Jesus told them, "You don't need to know about times or periods that the Father has determined by his own authority.*

The Kingdom of Israel that was set up by King David and King Solomon about 1,000 BC was destroyed by the Babylonian Empire in 586 BC. It came to life again as a nation about 70 years later but was conquered by the Roman general Pompey in 63 BC. It was then occupied by the army and became a province of the Roman Empire in 6 A.D. They set up a puppet king, King Herod, who was the ruler when Jesus was born.

Still, the Jews longed to have their own independent nation again, free of Roman control-----***the restored Kingdom of Israel***. That is why the disciples asked Jesus, "*Lord*, ***is this the time when you're going to restore the kingdom to Israel?***"

But Jesus didn't tell them, "*Don't be crazy, the future kingdom is in heaven*". No, he simply said they didn't need to know the exact time when the kingdom would be restored to Israel with Jesus as its King.

This is consistent with what the angel told Mary when it was announced to her that she would be the mother of Jesus----

Luk 1:30-31 GWv "*Don't be afraid, Mary. You have found favor with God. You will become pregnant, give birth to a son, and name him Jesus. He will be a great man and will be called the Son of the Most High.* ***The Lord God will give him the throne of his ancestor David. Your son will be king of Jacob's people*** [the Jewish people] ***forever, and his kingdom will never end.***"

King David's throne was ***a real throne in a real kingdom***----the Kingdom of Israel, and it is this kingdom that Christ will return to re-establish, and reign over ***forever*** from Jerusalem, except this time ***the kingdom will expand to include the whole Earth.***

But Jesus did give his followers some insight into what signs would exist on the Earth shortly before his Second Coming.

The Great Prophetic Sign---the Preservation of the Jewish People and their Eventual Return to the Land of Israel

God started out working with all peoples but because He gave humans freewill to make their own choices, things deteriorated and the Earth became filled with violence.

Because of this condition, God destroyed all living things on inhabited Earth by the great flood of Noah's day and **essentially started over with Noah and his family.**

Things began to deteriorate again so God narrowed things down to one particular man and his family-----the man Abraham. Abraham was a faithful man who lived in the large prosperous city of Ur in what is now modern Iraq. He was one of the very few people that still believed in the One True God.

God told him to pack up and leave Ur and ***go to a land that He would show to Abraham***. Abraham responded to God's request, left his prosperous life in Ur and went some 1500 miles to a new land----**the land of Canaan or what is now modern Israel and Palestine**.

Because of Abraham's faithfulness in following God's request for him to leave Ur, He made promises to Abraham, particularly that **Abraham and his descendants would inherit the land of Canaan (Israel) for an everlasting possession** and **that all nations would ultimately be blessed through Abraham**.

He was also promised that all this would work out through one of Abraham's special descendants, whom the New Testament identifies as the **Lord Jesus Christ**.

Because Abraham died in Canaan before he took possession of the land of Canaan, Jesus taught that Abraham must be resurrected and brought back to life so that he can personally receive all the land he was promised as an everlasting possession.

This is why God's promises to Abraham include **the promise of a resurrection from the dead**.

The apostle Paul tells us that all who believe and are baptized into Christ, become Abraham's heirs and are **likewise promised a resurrection from the dead.**

Gal 3:27 NLT *And all who have been united with Christ in baptism have put on Christ, like putting on new clothes...... And now that you belong to Christ,* ***you are the true children of Abraham. You are his heirs, and God's promise to Abraham belongs to you.***

Abraham's natural descendants through his son Isaac, and his grandson Jacob, **became the Jewish people and later the nation of Israel.** (Arab peoples are also descended from Abraham through his other son Ishmael)

God said that henceforth, **He would work to carry out His plan and purpose for the Earth through this one national group of people—the Jewish People and the Nation of Israel**---not because they are better than others, but only because of the faithfulness of one man, Abraham.

So, it was to this ethnic group that God gave His great moral law----the Ten Commandments---and it was through the Jewish people that He gave us most of His Word, thc Bible. That is, it was mainly Jewish people who received God's message and wrote it down for all of humanity.

He also chose the Jewish people to be the ethnic group through whom the Savior of the world would come-----Jesus Christ----since Mary, his mother, was Jewish.

In addition, He made the Jewish people the group **who** would be **His witnesses in the Earth to His very existence** due to the fact that through this people and their nation, Israel, He would carry out all His promises.

In addition, **He would preserve them as a distinct people and never allow them to be destroyed or lose their identity as Jews**.

Isa 43:10-11 GWv **"You** [the Jewish people and the nation of Israel] ***are my witnesses**," declares the LORD. "I have chosen you as my servant so that you can know and believe in me and understand* *that I am the one who did this. No god was formed before me, and there will be none after me. I alone am the LORD, and there is no savior except me.*

This is really quite remarkable because the Jews are the longest surviving distinct ethnic group on this planet. They have been a distinctive group for about 3500 years----unlike all other ancient peoples who lost their identity and disappeared.

Where are the ancient Romans, Babylonians, Assyrians, etc.? None of these other groups exists anymore, but the Jews have remained with their ancient beliefs, customs, and ancient language of Hebrew intact.

In addition, God told them that if they were faithful to His laws, He would bless them, and if they were unfaithful, He would curse them by expelling them from the land He gave them, and by scattering them all over the Earth.

Lev 26:33 NLT *I will scatter you among the nations and bring out my sword against you. Your land will become desolate, and your cities will lie in ruins.*

This happened the final time in A.D. 70 when the Roman general Titus captured Jerusalem from rebellious Jews in the Roman province of Judea, destroyed the city and the great Temple, and sent several million Jewish inhabitants throughout the Roman Empire, some as slaves.

They found that life was not pleasant for them in foreign lands. They had customs that were different from the rest of the population such as not eating pork products and circumcising their male infants. This made them stick out. As a result they experienced persecution.

Lev 26:36 GWv "*And for those of you who survive, I will demoralize you in the land of your enemies. You will live in such fear that the* *sound of a leaf driven by the wind will send you fleeing. You will run as though fleeing from a sword, and you will fall even when no one pursues you.*

But even though they were scattered and persecuted all around the Mediterranean Sea and into Europe, **they did not lose their identity as Jews** because God promised them that He would not allow them to be destroyed or lose their special identity.

Lev 26:44-45 GWv "*But despite all this, I will not utterly reject or despise them while they are in exile in the land of their enemies. I will not cancel my covenant with them by wiping them out, for I am the LORD their God.*

But then He made a follow-up promise: That as the end times approached, despite their earlier unfaithfulness, ***He would bring them back to their own land again and re-establish the Jewish nation of Israel on the same land as the ancient Kingdom of Israel.***

Eze 36:22-24 GWv "*Therefore, give the people of Israel this message from the Sovereign LORD:* ***I am bringing you back, but not because you deserve it.*** *I am doing it to protect my holy name, on which you brought shame while you were scattered among the nations...****For I will gather you up from all the nations and bring you home again to your land.***"

For centuries, this land (which came to be called Palestine), remained desolate with very few inhabitants. It was conquered by the Romans, then by the Arab Muslims, and finally by the Ottoman Turks, who made it into a wasteland, before it was finally liberated from the Ottoman Turks by the British in 1917 during World War 1.

After WW2 and the Holocaust in Nazi Germany where 6 million Jews were murdered, many of the remaining Jews in Europe went back to Israel and **a new nation of Israel came into being in 1948 and was approved by the United Nations**.

So the prophecy that the Jews would go back to their own land in the 'end times' became a reality some 75+ years ago.

Several wars with the surrounding Arab nations have happened since 1948 including in 1956 (Suez Crisis), in 1967 (Six-Day War when all of Jerusalem came under Israeli control), and in 1973 (Yom Kippur War), **but the Jewish nation was always victorious and has prospered**.

It is now home to 9 million people and is one of the most innovative and high-tech countries on this planet. It also has a very strong military despite its small size.

Jesus gave an important prophecy **about what we could expect regarding his Second Coming**, when Israel has come back into existence again as an independent nation and the Jewish people have returned to it from all over the world.

We will discuss this in the next chapter.

Day 43 Chapter 43: The Prophecy Jesus Gave About His Second Coming

After Jesus rose from the dead but before he ascended to his Father in heaven, he gave a final prophecy that included things about his Second Coming.

This prophecy was given in response to a question his disciples asked him: Mat 24:3 *"Tell us when all this will be," they asked, "and **what will happen to show that it is the time for your coming and the end of the age**?"*

Because his disciples asked him these questions when he was with them on the Mount of Olives, it is called the Olivet Prophecy.

Jesus understood their concerns so he took his time to give them a detailed answer.

But because the country had been conquered by the Roman Empire, and because the Romans were suspicious of any talk of a king or a kingdom that might appear to be a threat to Roman rule, Jesus used **symbolic language** in giving this prophecy. Otherwise, he could have been arrested by the Romans for treason.

So, he made his point by giving his answer ***in the form of a parable***. A parable is a story that also has another more hidden meaning.

In Matthew 24:32-35, Jesus said, "*Now **learn the parable from the fig tree...***" In other words, He makes it clear that while the story will be about a fig tree, it is really referring to something else.

The Jewish people knew that **the fig tree was a symbol of the nation of Israel.** It was a deciduous tree that grew everywhere in Israel, and most people had one in their yard (just like the maple leaf is a symbol of Canada).

So, his parable was really about **the nation of Israel**.

The same parable in the Gospel of Luke reads this way:

Luk 21:29-32 (GWv) *Look at the fig tree or any other tree.* As soon *as leaves grow on them, you know without being told that summer is near.* ***In the same way, when you see these things happen, you know that the kingdom of God is near.***

Luk 21:32 "I can guarantee this truth: ***This generation will not disappear until all this takes place.***

A fig tree loses its leaves in Winter and appears dead because it is a deciduous type of tree. But when its leaves burst forth in the Spring, it comes alive again.

What Jesus was telling them is that when you see the fig tree--- the nation of Israel--- come back to life again (after not existing for almost 2,000 years)----then know that the coming of ***"the Kingdom of God is near".***

Christ returns to earth so that he can set up the Kingdom of God all over the earth. Therefore, the **setting up of the Kingdom** and **the Return of Christ** are talking about the same time period**----**since one will happen right after the other.

Israel came back into being a nation again on May 15, 1948 following a resolution by the United Nations----the first time it was a nation again since the Roman conquest in 63BC and the destruction of the city of Jerusalem in AD 70 following a Jewish rebellion against Roman rule.

So, Jesus told his disciples, "*the generation that sees the 'rebirth' of that "fig tree" (nation of Israel)* ***shall not pass away till all these things take place***" (Matthew 24:32-35).

This then is the #1 sign that our Lord's return is near------ *the return of the Jewish people to their ancient homeland and the coming into existence again of the nation of Israel*_(after ceasing to exist for 2000 years).

Jesus said that **the generation that saw Israel become a nation again** would not completely disappear until "all this takes place"---namely, **the return of Christ and the setting up of the Kingdom of God.**

In the Bible, a "**generation" refers to an average human lifespan** at any given point in time (which in today's terms is about **80 years on average**). That means half the people die before age 80 and half die after age 80. So if the generation that was alive when Israel came back into being in 1948 hasn't passed before Christ returns, then Christ has to return in the next 10 to 15 years.

(This is the same time given for a generation in Psalm 90:10 (GNB) *Seventy years is all we have—**eighty years**, if we are strong; yet all they bring us is trouble and sorrow; life is soon over, and we are gone.*)

Based on the prophecy Jesus gave about the symbol of the fig tree, it appears that 1948 is when we start counting a generation (average human lifespan).

Over 75 years have already passed since the formation of the state of Israel in 1948. This likely means we should be very close to the return of Jesus to the Earth as the vast majority of people alive in 1948 will have died by age 90. (1948 + say, 90 yrs = 2038).

Consider what has changed since Israel's modern founding back in 1948. Israel today is a prosperous, secure, and very technologically advanced nation with a very strong military.

Jesus also said in this same prophecy in v. 24 (GWv) that "*Nations will trample Jerusalem* ***until the times allowed for the nations to do this are over***".

Since 1967 during the so-called Six Day War, Jerusalem has been in Israeli hands and is not controlled by other nations ***with one major exception: the sacred*** **Temple Mount** (the site of the ancient Jewish temple that was destroyed by the Romans in 70 AD) **is still controlled today by Arab Muslims**.

Therefore, this part of the prophecy has not been completely fulfilled because the most sacred site for Jews, **Temple Mount**, is still under the control of Muslims. It is the site of the ancient Jewish temple where a Muslim mosque, the Dome of the Rock, has been situated since 691 AD.

While the liberation of the ancient city of Jerusalem started in 1967, full liberation is not yet complete. That is why we we should be interested in any news events that involve the Temple Mount in Jerusalem.

The "*times of the Gentiles*" are still not over until the Temple Mount is back under full Jewish control.

This concludes our discussion of this greatest prophetic sign of the Second Coming of Christ. From this analysis, it would appear our Lord's return could come at any time now-----certainly within the next 20 years at the outside.

But there are also other signs which the Bible tells about that will occur near the time of the Second Coming of our Lord.

The disciples asked Jesus for multiple signs: "***Tell us the signs of your coming and the end of the age***" (Matthew 24:3). Jesus responded by giving them multiple signs to look for.

Then he added, "***When you see all these things, you can know my return is near. I'm right at the door.***" (Matthew 24:33 GWv).

He also said, "***When all these things begin to happen,*** *look up for* ***your salvation is near!***" (Luke 21:28 GWv).

What are "all these things"----these other signs?

These are the additional signs that Jesus said would all come together indicating events that would happen **just prior to his return back to earth.**

We will review what these additional signs are in the next chapter.

Day 44 – Chapter 44: Other Signs that Happen Close to When Christ Returns.

What are these other signs? Jesus and the prophets pointed to many signs but we will deal with only a few in this chapter. The reality of each one of these signs is undeniable and their "convergence" or coming together at one time should convince us that the return of Jesus is close at hand.

The most important sign is the one we discussed in the previous chapter: **the Jews back in their ancient land and the coming into being again of the Nation of Israel.**

The Jewish people, who have been scattered all over the earth since A.D. 70, were prophesied to return back to the land of Israel before Christ returns (Jeremiah 23:7-8). This has been fulfilled since the end of World War 2 and there are now more than 9 million people living in Israel.

Jesus gave some additional signs to look for in this same Olivet Prophecy:

1. **The Jewish People in Control of Jerusalem** - Jesus said armies would surround Jerusalem, destroy the city, and enslave its citizens. The Roman legions fulfilled this prophecy in A.D. 70. Since that time, foreign nations continued to control Jerusalem---the Crusaders, the Muslim Arabs, the Ottoman Turks, the British, and finally the Jordanians. As mentioned in the last chapter, this changed in 1967 when the Old City of Jerusalem was captured during the Six Day War and returned to Jewish control. **Since 1967, the Israelis have controlled the old city of Jerusalem except for Temple Mount.**

2. **The Gospel Preached Throughout the World** – Jesus said that the Gospel will be preached throughout the entire

world before his Second Coming so that every nation will hear it.

For centuries after the crucifixion, the Gospel was confined to a small area surrounding the Mediterranean Sea. In the past two centuries, Christians have brought the Gospel to every nation in the world. In addition, the Bible has been translated into hundreds of languages, and the message of Jesus is sent around the world by radio, TV, satellite, and the Internet.

As a result, this generation is on the verge of having spread the Gospel to every person on earth. This has never happened before now.

3. **An Increase in Travel and Knowledge** - Six hundred years before Jesus, an angel gave Daniel a special message. He said ***"travel and knowledge" will increase in a dramatic way at the end of the current age*** (Daniel 12:4).

   For centuries of human history, dramatic gains in travel and knowledge did NOT take place.

   Yet the last two hundred years, and particularly in the last 50 years since the arrival of jet air travel, we have witnessed great increases in widespread world travel. We have also seen great increases in the amount and availability of knowledge, particularly with the arrival of the internet. Hence, this prophecy has only been fulfilled in the last few years.

4. **The Arrival of Signs Close to Christ's Return would be like a woman experiencing birth pains.**

   Jesus said the appearance of many signs near to his return would be like a pregnant woman experiencing "birth pains" just prior to giving birth.

He said, (Matthew 24:3-8) Mat 24:8 GNB "*All these things are like the first pains of childbirth.*"

Birth pains (contractions) increase in frequency and intensity as a woman is close to giving birth.

This means **the frequency and intensity of these signs will increase as we near the actual return of Jesus back to earth**.

5. **Israel Surrounded by Enemies** - The Bible says enemies will surround Israel in the end times. Those enemies will say "*Come, let us wipe away the nation of Israel. Let's destroy the memory of its existence*" (Psalm 83:4 GWv) and "*Let us take for ourselves these pasturelands of God.*" (Psalm 83:12 GWv)

   Ezekiel said Israel's neighbors will falsely say, "*For you said, 'The lands of Israel and Judah will be ours. We will take possession of them. What do we care that the LORD is there!'* " (Ezekiel 35:10 NLT).

   Ever since the rebirth of Israel in 1948, Israel's Arab Muslim neighbors have claimed the land that made up ancient Israel for themselves, **without regard for what God has promised concerning the land of Israel.** He gave to the Jewish people the land of Israel as an everlasting inheritance in His promises to Abraham, thousands of years ago. This is why the Arab Muslim peoples have been unsuccessful in wars against Israel in 1948, 1956, and 1973-----and each time they were defeated.

   The latest war that began on October 7, 2023 when Hamas terrorists killed over 1200 Israeli civilians in a surprise attack, including babies and children, is just one more example of Israel's enemies who want to destroy the Jewish state. This will not happen.

6. **Israel's Strong Army---the IDF** - Ezekiel said, in the end times, Israel will field "*an exceedingly great army*" (Ezekiel 37:10). Zechariah said Israel will be like a fire among sheaves of grain, burning up the neighboring nations (Zechariah 12:6) and even the weakest Israeli soldier will be like David (Zechariah 12:8).

   Since 1948, Israel has fought no less than four conventional wars against its neighbors. Despite being outnumbered more than 50 to 1, Israel has achieved overwhelming victory every time and the **Israeli Defence Forces (IDF) is recognized as one of the top military forces on this planet**.

7. **Rise of the Gog of Magog Alliance** - The Bible prophecies that a military alliance of countries called **'Gog'** whose modern names include **Russia, Iran, and Turkey, and a number of Muslim nations---- will one day attack Israel** "*in the latter days*" (Ezekiel 38:8) after God brings His people home from foreign nations (Ezekiel 39:27)---something that has happened since the end of World War 2.

   Eze 38:14 "*Therefore, son of man,* ***prophesy against Gog****. Give him this message from the Sovereign LORD: When my people are living in peace in their land, then you will rouse yourself.*

   Eze 38:**15** ***You will come from your homeland in the distant north*** *with your vast cavalry and your mighty army,*

   Eze 38:16 *and you will attack my people Israel, covering their land like a cloud.* ***At that time in the distant future,***

I will bring you against my land as everyone watches, and my holiness will be displayed by what happens to you, **Gog**. *Then all the nations will know that I am the* LORD.

Today, we see those very nations coming together as allies for the first time - an alliance called 'Gog' and led by Russia that has never existed in world history.

The stage is being set right now for the **Gogian Invasion.** Putin may fit the description as the leader of ancient Magog who will lead this alliance.

8. **Denial of a Belief in Christ's return and a Decline in Christianity Generally-**
   Almost two thousand years ago, Peter issued a warning. He said in the last days people will mock the idea of Jesus returning. They will mock those who believe in the Second Coming and say exactly what we hear today - things like, " 2Pe 3:3-4 NLT *First, you must understand this: In the last days people who follow their own desires will appear.* ***These disrespectful people will ridicule God's promise by saying, "What's happened to his promise to return****? Ever since our ancestors died, everything continues as it did from the beginning of the world."* (2 Peter 3:3-4 NLT).

   In addition, Jesus predicted that Christianity itself would be in **decline.** Jesus asked the rhetorical question recorded in Luke 18:8 "*But when the Son of Man comes, will he find faith on earth?*" A rhetorical question is one that is not answered but where the answer is implied. The implied answer to this question asked by Jesus is that NO, Jesus will not find much faith when he returns because the Christian faith will be in serious decline. This is exactly what we see happening today.

Fewer and fewer people go to church or even claim to be Christians. Believing Christians are becoming a smaller and smaller group and their influence on culture and society is shrinking fast.

9. Rise of a United Europe - The Bible says a revived Holy Roman Empire will come to power in the end times (Daniel 2, Daniel 7, Revelation 17). According to Daniel, it will be an alliance of weak and strong nations. Some parts will be as strong as iron, while other parts will be as weak as clay (Daniel 2:42). We see the beginning of this alliance in the European Union - a coalition of weak and strong nations struggling to stay together.

To summarize, generations of Christians lived and died without witnessing any of these signs since most have only appeared in the last 50 years. For centuries of history, **none of these signs were present**. Today, **they nearly all are**.

Jesus said when you see "all these things" (signs), you can be assured that his return is near, in fact "right at the very door" (Matthew 24:33).

So, despite the skeptics, Jesus **is** coming **soon.** Even though we do not know the day, the hour, or year when he will return, it appears our era is very likely the era that will witness his return. The **coming together of all these signs at the same time** confirms it.

The prophet Daniel was given prophecy of what things would be like on the Earth just before the resurrection of the dead when Christ returns:

Dan 12:1 *It will be a time of trouble unlike any that has existed from the time there have been nations until that time. But at that time your people, everyone written in the book, will be rescued.*

Dan 12:2 *Many sleeping in the ground will wake up. Some will wake up to live forever, but others will wake up to be ashamed and disgraced forever.*

Here at the start of 2024 when this book is being published, it appears we may be entering this period. The world faces many challenges.

The USA may be facing the most chaotic election season in its entire history, multiple wars are erupting all over the planet, destructive natural disasters are becoming more frequent, global authorities are warning us to brace ourselves for the next pandemic, and our cities are being absolutely overwhelmed by endless waves of new migrants and homeless people.

Many are starting to think the stage is set for a societal implosion of epic proportions. Given all these signs, we should take the words of Jesus seriously:

Mat 24:33 " ... *when you see all these things, you know that he is near, at the door.*"

This should motivate every person to make the most of what time we have left to include God, the Eternal Lord of the Universe in our life every day, and become a follower of His Son, Jesus Christ.

Day 45 - Chapter 45: We All Make a Choice to Ignore God or to Include Him in Our Life. How Will You Choose?

Every person makes a choice either consciously or unconsciously at some point in their life to decide whether there is a God and whether they should include Him in their life, or ignore Him and act as if He doesn't exist and has no part of their life.

While God much prefers that we seek Him out and include Him as being important in our life, He will do nothing to force us to go down that road. If we wish to leave Him out of our life, He will allow us to do just that.

The consequence is that when we die, He will retain no memory of us and His promises will not include us. We will face everlasting destruction when we die.

Many are quite content with this outcome. They may conclude there isn't enough evidence for a loving God so they will just leave Him completely out of their lives. They may say they don't have enough interest or faith to pursue the matter any further.

That is the nature of faith in God. Faith always means there is a possibility of doubt; otherwise, it is not faith but fact. But God demands ***faith above all else*** from people---"*Without faith it is impossible to please Him. The man who approaches God must have faith in two things, first that God exists and secondly that God rewards those who search for him.* (Hebrews 11:6 ESV).

We are also told in **Eph 2:8** ESV "*For by grace you have been saved* ***through faith****. And this is not your own doing; it is the gift of God,*

From this reference, it is clear that first and foremost, **faith involves a belief that God actually exists** and that **He rewards those who seek Him out as an important part of their life**.

For some people, evidence of God's existence is perfectly clear as seen in the natural world---things like the fine pattern in a spider web, or the radar system that allows bats to fly in the dark. To many, these are evidence of a great Mind/Power/ Master Designer.

For others, what they see in a telescope in the heavens on a clear dark night or a microscope can be explained in purely naturalistic terms without any need for a super human Mind and Power.

Whether we see evidence for God in the natural order and in His dealings with us, or whether we don't, ***is a matter of our own choice.*** God doesn't force us to believe that He exists but He wants very much for us to have faith that He does exist.

Faith is a combination of two things:

1. **Belief**----things you accept that are true about something or someone
2. **Trust**----whether the person or organization are trustworthy and will do what they have promised to do

Both these things are necessary regarding faith in the God of the Bible.

Regarding **BELIEF**, He requires that we believe that.....

1. He exists
2. He is the Creator and Sustainer of the Universe
3. He is a moral Being and the Source of Moral Laws---the Ten Commandments
4. He has a plan and purpose for creating humans on this earth and history is moving to the climax when this plan

will be brought into being when His son Jesus Christ returns to Earth and sets up the worldwide Kingdom of God.

5. All people answer to Him for the choices they make in their life.

Regarding **TRUST**, He requires that we trust that He will ***perform the things He has promised*** for those people who Believe in Him, and Respect Him by including Him in their life and trying to keep His moral laws.

His promises to those who believe in Him and seek after Him----focus on **three things**:

1. His *promise to forgive us of our sins*
2. His *promise to raise us from the dead* at the time when His Son returns to Earth to set up the Kingdom of God.
3. His *promise to give us an immortal eternal existence here on earth in the Kingdom of God.*

If we choose to seek after God, He wants us to put some effort into this relationship. **It is not something that will happen automatically by default.** If a person is interested in a hobby or another person, they will commit some time and effort to that interest. God is no different.

That may be why He has chosen to be partially hidden from human beings. **He has made His existence not so obvious. It is not "in our face"** and we have to search it out. As a result, belief in Him is not automatic. It still requires searching, reflection, and faith.

Faith can only exist when there is some doubt. *If we have the option of believing, then we must also have the option of not believing.*

So, it appears that **just enough evidence exists to convince those who *want* to believe in God's existence**, but not enough evidence exists to make it overwhelming for those who have no interest in believing.

Pure reason alone cannot determine the choice we make.

The more evidence we have of God's existence, the less need there is for faith. Therefore, God is not "in our face"; **He remains somewhat distant and hidden so that we have to put time and effort into searching Him out.**

This isn't the way most people like things to be. Most people **like to have certainty**. We like to know that God exists for certain and that everything I have been telling you about God's plans for this Earth are 100% certain to happen.

But **God doesn't work this way**. He knows that if we were certain about these things, it would make us arrogant and full of pride. As are result, **He does not give us certainty,** but He will give us enough information for us to reflect on and make a reasoned choice that He does exist and that the things He has promised are true.

So, **if we choose** to see the hand of God in the world around us as well as in our own lives, ***then we will be able to do so***.

Likewise, if we want to deny the hand of God in the natural world, in overseeing world events, or in His plan for us and for the Earth, we can come up with enough doubts to do so. That is the way faith in God works.

It all comes down to how we understand of what we observe in the world or have experienced, which is also affected to some extent by ***what we want to believe.*** To believe in the personal God of the Bible involves some faith.

But to reject the personal God of the Bible also involves faith, as we discussed in an earlier chapter when we talked about Pascal's wager.

So, every person makes this choice at some point---consciously or unconsciously----and the choice they make influences their thinking (by means of their worldview), their behavior, their hopes for the future, and their future destiny.

How will you choose?

Jesus made it plain that ***most people will not choose to seek after God and His Son Jesus Christ***. They prefer to go their own way and hope for the best.

Jesus described things this way (Matt 7: 13-14 Voice version)

"There are two paths before you; you may take only one path. One doorway is narrow. And one door is wide.

Go through the narrow door. For the wide door leads to a wide path, and the wide path is broad; the wide, broad path is easy, and the wide, broad, easy path has many, many people on it; but the wide, broad, easy, crowded path leads to death.

[14] *Now then that narrow door leads to a narrow road that in turn leads to life. It is hard to find that road. Not many people manage it."*

Jesus is making it clear that seeking after God requires we take the narrow road and **this requires effort on our part because as he says, "*it is hard to find that road.*"**

But you ***can*** find that road and then take it. It just requires some searching and reflection to seek it out.

Day 46 -Chapter 46: Take Hold of that *Good Plan* God Has *for You*--- for a Better Life *Now* and a *Future* Filled With Hope

At the beginning of this book, I stated that you and I were put on this Earth for a good purpose that only each one of us can fulfill and that God sometimes allows us to screw-up because ***it is often the only way He can get our attention when we have been living a life without Him.***

That is why I hope you will consider changes in the direction of your life so that you can find that true good purpose that He wants for you and that only you can fulfill.

But this in turn depends on your willingness to take control of your life and particularly, control of your thinking and actions----and move them in different direction.

I have argued in this book that the best way to start moving along a new path is to adopt a Biblical Worldview as the basis for your thinking and for the choices you make.

Just to review again, the Biblical Worldview includes the following ideas: that.....

- There is a God that brought the universe including human beings into existence;
- This Being had a purpose for creating the universe including the Earth including humans;
- He communicated this purpose to people in what we call God's Word, or the Bible;
- God is working out His plan through what is called the Gospel or Good News about the coming Kingdom of God here on Earth and Salvation from eternal destruction;

- God recognizes every human being as a person of value because every person is made in His image, that He had a good purpose for bringing each of us this world;

- Every person needs Salvation from everlasting destruction of their existence at death because in our native state from birth, we are separated from God and are without hope;

- Salvation means I will have all my sins forgiven and after I die, God will remember me so that I will be resurrected, judged with grace, and receive a new immortal existence in that Kingdom of God here on Earth;

- This is all made possible by the death of Jesus Christ, God's only begotten Son----our Savior and future King, who died for the sins of all people.

If this Worldview seems reasonable to you, then all that is needed is a commitment to change your ***outlook and behavior***. Even if you backslide sometimes, as long as you are trying to move your life in another direction, Jesus Christ----our Lord, Judge, and future King----will do the rest and make up the difference.

Day 47 - Chapter 47: The Benefits Now of Making A Change

We read earlier that God promises to reward those who seek after Him and include Him in their life.

Many people choose not to make Him an important part of their life. And, He has no interest in forcing a person to include Him in their life. It must be a voluntary freewill choice.

But for those who seek after Him and make Him an important part of their lives, things are different. **He does remember them and promises to reward them**.

There are different types of rewards that God promises to those who are willing to change course and go down a different path---some develop now and some are future.

When a person commits to become a follower of the Lord Jesus, there are a number of benefits that can begin to happen. A person.......

- ....should begin to see his life as having more purpose with a reason for living, even if you remain in prison for some time;
- ...should begin to lose the feeling that he has little to contribute as a person because of past screw-ups;.... should begin to have better, more trusting relationships with other people as they recognize he has changed course and is going down a different path;
- .....should begin to feel less burdened down with negative feelings of guilt, shame, and a life of regret because those things relate to his old life and have been put behind him.

In addition, those who include God in their life and want to be followers of His Son Jesus Christ are regarded as God's **"agents"** for good in the world.

An agent is one who acts on behalf of another person. That is, when one person prays to God and asks for some form of help, that help often comes by means of another person----even though that other person may be completely unaware that he is acting as God's agent.

For example, if you were acting as "mentor" by trying to help another prisoner who was in a bad way mentally, you might be fulfilling such a role.

It doesn't matter what your past is or what you look like. God is only concerned with the **change----*the change inside you*----**in your mind, your heart, and your thinking.

A special blessing is given to those who help others turn from a life of evil. In the book of James, we read,

"My brothers and sisters, if one of you wanders from the truth, someone can bring that person back. Realize that whoever brings a sinner back from the error of his ways *will save him from death, and many sins will be* **forgiven. (James 5: 19-20 GWv)**

Changing course is a big decision that some other prisoners you currently associate with may not understand or approve of so that such change may not be comfortable for you at the start.

The Bible is full of accounts about real people who screwed up badly, but, with God's help, were able to turn things around in a positive way.

So, like every other person, **you have a decision to make:**

1. To continue just as you are and leave the Eternal Lord God and His Son out of your life.

2. To make a change in your thinking, outlook, and relationship to God and His Son by including them in your thinking and your choices.

This is a strictly private matter between you, God, and His Son Jesus Christ.

May you make the choice that is best for you.

Day 48 - Chapter 48: Become Part of that 'Band of Brothers" who Serve Jesus as Lord and Soon Coming King

If you decide to go down this new path, you should consider **taking the final step** and undergo water baptism if this is possible for you at your facility.

As we discussed in an earlier chapter, **baptism is the outward sign of your genuine commitment to change the direction of your life and follow a new path**.

- When you rise from the water, it is as if you have died and been buried with Christ **so that you come out a new man in Christ Jesus** with your sins forgiven and your relationship with the Lord of the Universe and His Son Jesus Christ, forever changed.
- In baptism, you symbolically "die" and share in Christ's death **so that you can also share in His resurrection**.
- **You are declared "righteous" and your sins and past crimes are forgiven**.
- Jesus Christ is now your true Lord You so that you become a brother "in Christ" and are adopted into God's covenant people. By doing so you qualify as an heir of all God's promises. As we indicated in an earlier chapter, this ceremony is a public declaration that you are putting your old way of life behind you. It provides a way for you to declare that you are making a formal break with your past and all its sins.

To review again, you need to seek out the prison chaplain and tell him that you want to be baptized. You tell him that you have repented of your sins, that you believe the gospel message, and acknowledge Jesus Christ as your Lord and Savior.

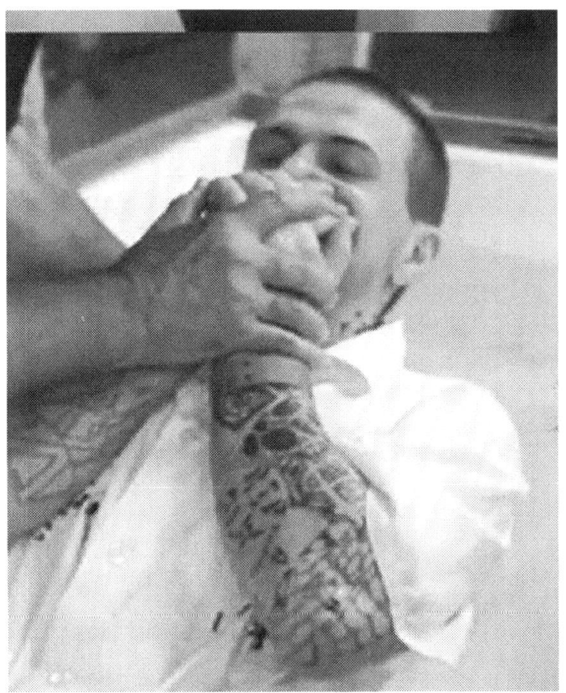

Prisoner being baptized in prison (photo source could not be traced or attributed at publishing date)

At the baptism ceremony, the chaplain will briefly acknowledge these things about your beliefs and then submerge your whole body in the tank of water. That is all there is to it.

You are now beginning a journey as a "new man in Christ Jesus". This lifts a great psychological burden for you and will greatly improve your outlook and mental health **because you now have the confidence that the Lord Jesus Christ has paid the price for your sins.**

You can then begin your life as a 'new man'----a life of hope and promise----where your crimes no longer define who you are or determine your future destiny.

The challenge for every person after being baptized is to follow through and demonstrate a genuine commitment to this new life. There are things you can do each day to help you on this new journey:

- **Talk to God every day---- It is a private matter between you and God**. Ask Him to help you get through the day. Talk to Him as a man talks to a friend who cares about how you are doing. Thank Him for any positive things that happened in your day. Tell Him about any challenges you face that day. Ask Him to give you wisdom and help you keep His commandments so you will make good choices.

- **Take One Day at a Time** because changing your thinking and automatic response to situations doesn't come easy for anyone. For example, every day, **try to do what is right for that day** by not breaking any of God's moral laws---no lying, cheating, stealing from, or harming others.

- **Try to read something spiritual every day and check out for yourself whether you think the things I have discussed in this book are true.** (including re-reading parts of this book which I hope you will keep as a reference).

- It is also highly recommended to read the Bible itself. If you don't have a Bible, ask the prison chaplain if he can get you one (preferably a version in modern English). Start with reading about Jesus' life in the gospels of Matthew, Mark, Luke or John. These accounts also tell us how Jesus treated other people and how he wants us to act towards others. Then read the book of Acts, which comes right after the gospels, and tells about the spread of the gospel in the Roman Empire. Then read the first book of the Bible, Genesis. It tells us about the Creation, the Fall of Adam, How God interacted with people in ancient times and the principles He gave for interacting with Him. It also tells us about the promises He made to Abraham, Isaac, and Jacob---promises that we all can share in. Lastly, read some of the Psalms. They can helpful when you need encouragement or comfort.

- **Follow world events----particularly those that involve Israel and the city of Jerusalem**, **particularly the Temple Mount**; also, any news items involving Russia, Iran, Turkey, and other Arab nations. These are all involved in end-time prophecies about the Second Coming of Jesus back to earth.

- **Seek out other prisoners who may be more in line with your new way of thinking** so you can keep a more positive outlook. Just be aware that some may not be genuine and are leading you on for some other negative reason.

- If you feel comfortable, **consider attending a Bible study group** in prison where you can express your thoughts on what the Bible means to you. It will help you learn more, stimulate your thinking and give you some association with other more like-minded prisoners.

- When you become part of that 'band of brothers' that serve the Lord Jesus, you become a representative of all that Jesus stands for. If you have the opportunity and feel comfortable, share with other prisoners who may be feeling down on themselves, in a quiet casual way, **the change you made in your life and how it has helped you.**

In conclusion, I came across these words in a recent book I read that I really liked and that are applicable to everyone:

"*Don't miss out on what God is going to do. He doesn't want you to waste your life. He wants you to be part of something that is far bigger than most people can even imagine, but it is up to you to embrace that plan.*

In life, everyone gets knocked down at some point.

But those that refuse to stay down are the ones that end up being victorious.

Don't let your past keep you from the future that you are supposed to have. God can make a way where there seems to be no way.

If you give everything to Him, He will take the broken pieces of your life and turn them into a beautiful thing, and He will help you live a life that really matters [even in prison—RT]"
---Snyder, Michael, 7 Year Apocalypse, Amazon Digital Services

The Apostle Paul wrote these words to the new believers at Corinth, a notoriously evil seaport city (2 Cor, 5:15-18)

"*Since we believe that Christ died for all, we also believe that we have all died to our old life. He died for everyone so that those who receive his new life will no longer live for themselves. Instead, they will live for Christ, who died and was raised for them.*

This means that anyone who belongs to Christ ***has become a new person. The old life is gone****; a new life has begun!*

And all of this is a gift from God, who brought us back to himself through Christ. And God has given us this task of reconciling people to him."

In conclusion, I hope you will keep this book as a reference and read it over and over with the hope that it will help make you that better human being you are called to be.

And may the Eternal Lord of the Universe bless you on this new journey with a true good destiny that He has badly wanted for you since you were born, despite all the mis-steps and challenges you have faced.

I conclude with this Biblical prayer: **Num 6:24 NLT**
May the LORD bless ***you*** *and take care of* ***you****; May the LORD be kind and gracious to you; May the LORD look on* ***you*** *with favor and give* ***you*** *peace.*

Long-term Prisoner's Prayer

Eternal Lord, the King of the Universe, May all praise, honor, and glory be given to Your Name for ever and ever.

I thank you for this new day of life and health. Keep me safe and in health this day as my great Protector, Provider and Healer.

Help me with any challenges I face today by giving me **wisdom** so that I am able to make wise choices that are both right and good.

Help me to accept *the things I **cannot** change* like my imprisonment but give me peace to deal with them in a positive way so they don't drag me down.

Help me change the things I ***can*** change like rejecting criminal thinking and following a Christian worldview so I can transform my thinking and actions to a better way.

I acknowledge You as the Source of all moral laws----like the Ten Commandments---and confess that in the past I disregarded or rebelled against You and Your commandments, and recognize that my criminal acts, where I chose to do what I knew was wrong, were first and foremost a sin against You.

Help me to take responsibility for my part in the criminal acts I was convicted of and to not blame others for my choices.

Help me to recognize the grief and harm I caused to my victim(s), their families, and to my own family. Bring them healing and comfort.

Help me to accept that my imprisonment by the state is Your will because You have given authority to the state to punish wrongdoing. But help me to use my time in prison in useful, productive ways.

Help me to be your agent for good while I am in prison---to encourage, build up, and give hope to others---- when I see a need and have an opportunity.

Restore me to Your good favour and help me to become that better human being You are calling me to be so I can move forward with my life in prison in a positive way and fulfil that good plan You have for me.

Lastly, grant me a place in your soon coming Kingdom under the just rulership of my Lord, Savior, and Soon Coming King, the Lord Jesus Christ, through whom I ask this prayer. Come Lord Jesus! Amen.

Bibliography and Recommended Reading

For additional reading, all the books and videos listed below are excellent resources which helped the author gain many valuable insights in completing this book.

Brown, Brene, Various talks by this researcher dealing with Shame, Guilt, and Vulnerability (available on YouTube)

Colson, Charles, Justice That Restores, Tyndale House Publishers, Inc. Wheaton IL, 2001

Colson, Charles, and Pearcey, Nancy, The Problem of Evil, Tyndale House Publishers Inc., Wheaton, IL, 1999

Drucker, Ernest, A Plague of Prisons, The New Press, New York, 2011

D'Souza, Dinesh, What's So Great About Christianity, Regnery Publishing , Inc., Washington, D.C., 2007

Gilder, George, Men and Marriage, Pelican Publishing Company, Gretna, La., 1986

Gilligan, James M.D., Violence: Our Deadly Epidemic and Its Causes, G. P. Putnam's Sons, New York, 1996

Popenoe, David, Life Without Father, Martin Kessler Books - The Free Press, New York, 1996

Prager, Dennis, Genesis, God Creation and Destruction, The Rational Bible, Regnery Faith, Washington, 2019

Samenow, Stanton E. PhD, Inside the Criminal Mind, Times Books, Random House, New York, 1984

Rainey, Dennis, A Call to Courageous Manhood, Trail Life, 2021

Wilson, James Q., and Herrnstein, Richard J. , Crime and Human Nature: A Definitive Study of the Causes of Crime, Simon and Schuster, New York, 1985

Acknowledgments

I am grateful to the publishers of the modern translations of the Bibles listed below for allowing me to use quotations from their respective versions of the Bible within the copyright provisions that each allow. These include:

English Standard Version (ESV) copyright, 2005 Crossway Bibles, a publishing ministry of Good News Publishers, Wheaton IL, USA

Good News Bible (GNB), copyright, 1976 American Bible Society, published by Harper Collins,

God's Word Version (GWv), publisher and copyright, God's Word to the Nations Mission Society, 1995 to 2020

New Living Translation (NLT), publisher and copyright, Tyndale House Translation, 1996 to 2015

The Voice, (Voice V.) , publisher and copyright,
Thomas Nelson, 2008, 2011

Author Contact Info

Deveron Books

P.O. Box 71, Drumbo Postal Outlet

69 Oxford St. W

Drumbo ON Canada N0J 1G0

I am a retired former college teacher and do volunteer work with a restorative justice program for young offenders. I reside in Ontario, Canada. I welcome comments from readers and will respond by regular mail or Jpay email (where available) or by messaging using GTL Gettingout (where available) or GTL Network (where applicable). The author's contact name will appear as rfarrar. I will not answer requests for money.

Appendix A

Twelve Tips from Former Inmates to Help Make Your Imprisonment More Tolerable

It is almost impossible to avoid all possible trouble in prison. However, if you follow the Twelve Tips given below from experienced prisoners, you have a good chance of minimizing your encounters with trouble. Being in prison is like being in a constant state of war. That is why you need to take prudent steps to minimize bad encounters and outcomes. (This list was adapted from multiple source)

1. **Mind Your Own Business: Don't Ask About the Crimes or Private Lives of Other Inmates or Don't Tell About Your Own**. **Avoid Arguments**. Mind your own business. In other words don't get involved in things that do not concern you. Avoid any discussion with another inmate that seems headed for an argument----which can in turn lead to resentment and violence. If another inmate feels comfortable with you and wishes to share things about himself, that is ok but don't try to encourage it. Likewise, if you feel comfortable with another inmate such as your cellie and wish to reveal the nature of your crime or things about your private life, that is ok as well. But do it only after you know another inmate pretty well. This is particularly true for crimes of a sexual nature or ones involving children when nothing should be revealed.

2. **Stay Clear of Gambling and Gambling Debts** Learning a few card games to pass the time is one thing. Card games involving gambling or any other type of gambling can quickly become a "no win situation" where you could be putting your life in danger. There are two serious

consequences of gambling: 1. You don't have the money to pay your gambling debts, or, 2. You win at gambling but the wrong people very angry. Prisoners have little tolerance in collecting gambling debts and will quite quickly resort to violence against you or make your life hell on Earth when you owe them.

3. **Stay Clear of Prison Gangs** Joining a prison gang may seem like a good option when you first come to prison----for protection and for people to hang out with. However, there is a steep price to be paid when you join a prison gang. The gang basically owns you and will demand that you do things you may not want to do to prove your loyalty. Most of these things could land you in a lot of trouble. And trying to leave a prison gang may be nearly impossible. So, just stay clear of prison gangs all costs.

4. **Treat Prison Guards With Respect but Never Side with them, Never get friendly with one of them, and Never Share Information with them about other prisoners. Silence is the best policy----always.** Otherwise, you risk being labelled as a snitch----a very dangerous position to put yourself in so avoid it at all costs. It is the single most damaging thing you can do to your reputation while in prison. So, do not snitch and do not talk to a guard unless someone is with you . Even then do not carry on idle conversations with staff.

5. **Be Very Wary of Anyone Who Wants to Befriend You or Take You "Under Their Wing" or Do Favors for you.** Particularly when you are first incarcerated. They may be trying to coerce youinto a sexual relationship to be their "punk" in return for protection or other favors. In time, you will get to know other inmates whom you can trust that have no ulterior motives in associating

with you. And never accept gifts from anyone in prison because such gifts almost always come with some form of obligation you won't be aware of at the time and most of which you won't like.

6. **Do not become indebted to Anyone** Purchase only things you can afford to buy and never take things that belong to other inmates. To do so could get you killed or seriously injured. If you need money, try to set up some kind of "hustle"----performing services for other inmates like doing their laundry, fixing or repairing things, etc.

7. **Walk with Your Head Up, Your Eyes Straight Ahead and Avoid Staring or Making Direct Eye Contact with inmates you don't know or may fear some reason.** Many inmates are very sensitive to pick up on any perceived slight including what may appear to them to be you staring at them. This can quickly turn to violence. Do not walk down the walk looking into cells . But never have your head down so that it appears you are looking at the floor either. That makes you appear weak and defeated and hence vulnerable. Instead, keep your head up so that you look alert and confident with your eyes straight ahead.

8. **Avoid Using Drugs or Making/Consuming Prison Booze** It is well known that illicit drugs are readily accessible in prison, particularly through prison gangs. Stay clear of these things as they are a guaranteed road to trouble. There are multiple risks: You may become indebted for your drugs and then addicted, which only compounds the problem. And you risk being caught in a shakedown and then punished. The short-term relief that drug use may bring is not worth the long-term pain-----being placed in segregation or being sent to a tougher maximum

security prison. Drug use and trouble go together so just stay clear of drugs or prison made hooch

9. **Keep Occupied and Work Out Regularly** Keep occupied doing things and do not think about the free world 24/7 by having a daily routine including a fitness routine or working out with weight training. It helps maintain your physical health and helps pass the time. It is also good for your mental health and weight training can help to bulk you up so that you do not appear weak or vulnerable. – making you less of a target by other inmates.

10. **Avoid Getting 'Inked Out' With lots of Visible Prison Tattoos** Because many prisoners have multiple prison tattoos, new inmates often think this is a good way to become accepted and fit in. However, prison tattoos are often a visible sign that you wish to be associated with the criminal prison culture and its thinking. It is also one of the most common ways for transmitting bad diseases like hepatitis C, a very serious liver disease that is rampant in prison. Most inmates also regret prison ink once they are released since many prison tattoos depict anti-social symbols (skulls, swastikas, spider webs, etc.) that are associated with criminals and prison. Also, most tattoos don't age well-----they start 'bleeding' and lose their sharp form in a few years. What often results is an ugly, crude-looking mass of blue/black ink that forever marks you as a convicted felon.

11. **Be respectful and polite to Other Inmates** Respect is the one thing a prisoner has that he values. Any inmate who tries to take that away from him is looking for trouble. Do not call anyone names like b*tch or punk unless you are prepared to fight and do not let anyone call you those names Even very small things can be perceived as

showing disrespect. So always be respectful and polite to other prisoners. If you show respect to other inmates, they will likely show respect to you. Why would you want to create enemies in prison?

12. **Try to Maintain Contact With Family and Friends to Avoid Feeling Isolated and Alone** This sometimes easier said than done as contact with family and friends may fade away over time. However, family are still important and hopefully can give you support and give you a lifeline outside of prison.

13. **Do Not Point.** No pointing with your fingers. Don't point at the sky, the ground, the guy getting killed over yonder, the inmate escaping over the kill fence, Don't Point Ever. Reason is simple: That probably innocent gesture of yours can and will be taken so out of context by everyone inside the walls, all of them will be certain you are pointing at, thus talking about, and discussing, that inmate. And you will swiftly get your come-uppance, if you will, for that terrible misdeed.

Appendix B

Personal Non-Denominational Statement of My Basic Beliefs (Modeled on the Content of the **Apostle's Creed**) *

**The Apostles' Creed is one of the oldest documents that could qualify as a Statement of Essential Christian Beliefs. It reflects the thinking closer to the times of the apostles regarding what concepts were important to be believed. As a result, I have modelled this non-sectarian Statement of Basic Beliefs, which reflects my own understanding, on the content of this very old document.*

I believe in One God-- the self-existent Eternal Father, the Creator and Sustainer of heaven and earth, and the ultimate first cause; He is an all-powerful, infinite, omniscient, omnipresent, invisible, immortal Spirit; He is a God of love---- ' merciful, gracious, slow to anger'; ' He loves righteousness and justice, and is a God of truth' ; 'He gives to all, life, breath and all things', He ' made from one blood every nation', is 'no respecter of persons', and is desirous that all people should seek after Him. Hence, He has a personal interest in human beings who acknowledge that He exists, He hears their prayers, and is a 'rewarder of those who diligently seek Him*

I believe in Jesus Christ, the only begotten son of the Eternal Father, the promised Messiah, and our Lord, who was conceived by the Holy Spirit, and, being " *born of a woman*", "*he also himself likewise took part of the same*"--- the same unclean, sin-prone human nature common to all the descendants of Adam; "*he learned obedience by the things that he suffered*' and "*was tempted in all ways like unto us, but without sin*" , he suffered under Pontius Pilate, was crucified, died, and was buried, rose from the dead on the third day, was seen alive by many witnesses, and ascended to heaven to sit at the right hand of the Eternal Father, and, as "*Jesus Christ the human*" -GWv)--- is the Mediator between God and man, from whence he shall return to the Earth as Judge and King of Kings.

I believe in the Holy Spirit, God's power used to accomplish His will and fulfil His purpose----particularly in bringing salvation and providing support and comfort to those who are called by Him and respond to that call. There is unity of purpose between the One God and Father, His son Jesus Christ, and in the operation of the Holy Spirit.

I believe God accurately communicated to human beings all necessary information regarding His plan and purpose, and moral laws to promote right living and an orderly society---- **by giving us His Inspired Word, the Bible**, conveyed through human intermediaries, who wrote at the prompting and oversight of the Holy Spirit.

I believe the Gospel-----the central focus of all that God has promised in His Word-- -which is the **good news of "*the things concerning the Kingdom of God and the Name of Jesus Christ,*"** and "*the power of God unto salvation to everyone that believes*".

> **The "Things concerning the Kingdom of God "** are about a real kingdom that will be set up here on Earth by its King, Jesus Christ, at his Second Coming, at which time, dead believers will be raised. Following the judgement, he will extend the Kingdom over the whole Earth by subduing and judging the existing nations and their inhabitants. He will reign from Jerusalem as King of Kings over the whole Earth. During the 1000 year millennial reign of Christ, the whole Earth will be restored to its original

Edenic state. At the end of this period, the curse, sin, and death will be abolished, and God will be "all in all".

The "Things Concerning the Name of Jesus Christ" relate to his great redemptive work in dying on the cross for our sins and then being raised to life. Those who accept Him as our resurrected Lord and Savior and are baptized into His saving name, qualify to receive God's promises as an act of grace.

I believe the Church is the one" body of Christ", a worldwide community (assembly) of believers with Christ as its head, whose mission is to be a light in a dark world by upholding the faith, preaching the gospel, supporting the needy, and collectively implementing the teachings of our Lord in daily life.

I believe all human beings (including our Lord) while made in the image of God, are born into the condemned line of Adam and inherit a mortal nature called "sin in the flesh"----an unclean state that separates us from God and that causes a natural inherited tendency within us to want to choose evil so that we inevitably become sinners by actual transgression, which further separates us from God. In this separated state, we are without hope and destined for permanent destruction of our being unless saved by grace. Only Jesus our Lord was perfectly obedient in overcoming this evil tendency and committed no sins.

I believe grace is extended to us by God on the basis of our faith---namely, belief and trust in God and in His promises, and in the resurrection of the Lord Jesus, followed by repentance of our sins, baptism into our Lord's saving name, and an ongoing commitment to implement his teachings and example in our lives. This involves first and foremost, loving God and loving our neighbor as ourselves so we can do what is just and good.

In so doing, we live in hope of a resurrection because we have associated ourselves with our Lord's death and resurrection through our baptism. In addition, our sins are forgiven, we enter into a new covenant relationship with the Eternal Father as His adopted sons and daughters, and as brothers and sisters of our Lord, and qualify as heirs of His promises.

Made in the USA
Columbia, SC
21 October 2024